SECOND TIME FOSTER CHILD

What Others are Saying About...

SECOND TIME FOSTER CHILD

Toni Hoy has been forced into the corner in a way that few on the planet have ever had to experience. Her book details what she rightly terms her "Devil's Deal" and the way it has ripped at the fabric of her family. Forced to choose between profound family and personal pain in order to care for her child, or an easy way out, she chose pain. She chose to save her son. Whether you will ever be in her situation or not, you need to read this book. It may change the way you view benevolent government intervention, forever. It may change the way you look at case workers, who come professing their desire to help. It will certainly change the way you look at your family, and if you let it, it will change the depth of your love.

Ken Huey, Ph.D, CEO CALO
(Change Academy Lake of the Ozarks), Lake of the Ozarks, MO

Second Time Foster Child is a must read for anyone who has experienced the mental/behavioral health system on any level! It's a close as you can get to "been there, done that" when fighting for health care for a child with mental/behavioral illnesses. I don't know of any family, or family member, who wouldn't be able to relate to this story! Toni Hoy has bared her heart and soul with her inner strength to give a VOICE, not only to her family, but families across the country! She is an inspiration for every mother of a mentally/behavioral challenge child!

Mary Thunker, President, A.S.K. (Alphabet Soup Kids), Omaha, NE

Toni Hoy's *Second Time Foster Child* challenges professionals in child welfare and juvenile justice systems to examine their practices, and to answer some tough, but fair questions. This book offers a refreshingly candid look at what happens to mentally and physically disabled children and their families, who are looking for support. A compelling, gripping, personal journey told from the perspective of a mother who faces brutal choices, and continues to love her son…

Laurie Jarvis, Advocate, Speaker & Writer, St. Paul, MN

Toni Hoy is a child and family advocate par excellence. Her personal story of her battle to save her family and her son is not just her story: she both beautifully and strategically weaves her own family's heartbreaking experience into the context of the needs of children and families, generally. She demonstrates over and over that the social policies that are meant to protect children and preserve families that have been tragically obeyed in the breach, time after time, exactly when children's and families' needs are greatest. If ever one family's story can be the occasion for changing what ails our social services, mental health and family/juvenile court systems, to make those systems responsive to the child and his need for family connections, this story will do it. Thank you Toni Hoy!

Diane Redleaf, Executive Director, Family Defense Center, Chicago, IL

I've been reading Toni Hoy's blog and learning a lot about her experiences and her state's child welfare system. Nothing I had read prepared me for this moving story of a close family, the accommodations made, and the lessons learned in how to rear these children. Toni walks us through the experience of having foster children with undiagnosed mental illness, why the system has imploded, and how she and her husband have fought for help for their kids. Their joys and struggles are moving and heart-wrenching. Toni does not sugar-coat the difficulties and sacrifices of each family member and their resulting successes and happiness. This is an inspirational story that will help you understand the complex issues and will make you want to help fix the system for others.

Marcia Stein, PHR, CA, author of
Strained Relations: Help for Struggling Parents of Troubled Teens

Toni Hoy bares her soul in this courageous true story of her family's journey to help and heal her severely traumatized adopted son. Determined to make a difference for others, and assure true "forever families" for adopted children, Toni bravely forges ahead in her crusade to right the wrongs in seeking mental health treatment for adopted children, without having to trade custody rights.

Michael Groomer, Founder and Beverly Hansen, Executive Director,
Advocates for Children of Trauma, Fort Worth, TX

Toni delivers a moving, first-hand account of the life of a secondary survivor going up against an out-dated and misguided legal system. Her unending determination to support her two boys through their recovery from pre-adoptive trauma clearly depicts the courage and dedication required, to help a survivor survive. For the professional and layperson alike, looking for more insight on trauma recovery, her story offers us a riveting, easily digestible, and educational glimpse into the real life of a child with post-traumatic stress. Trauma survivors from many walks of life as well as their friends and family, who have ever had to tangle with the legal system, will recognize similar challenges on these pages and find hope in her eventual success-reminding us that through our collective efforts we will eventually reach our goal of improving trauma services for survivors and their families.

Jessica Olson, President, DartHeart Inc., Hanover, NH

We are overwhelmed by sadness when we hear continuing stories from parents of how their love, concern, and words are used against them and their child, by a system that is supposed to serve and protect those very families. *Second Time Foster Child* helps us to see how and why this system must be changed; in the author's words...'I want (my son) not to ever have a smidgen of doubt that he's worth it.' Nearly 500,000 other children in Foster Care in the U.S. each year are worth it, too!

Diana Waggoner, Executive Director, Kim Foundation, Omaha, NE

A much needed expose of our broken child welfare system. DCFS views all families with the same lens. All parents are assumed to be child abusers and negligent. They do not know how to treat dysfunctional children in normal families! It is imperative that parents have access to services for their emotionally and mentally ill children. Through their tax dollars they pay for those governmental services but cannot access them when they are in need. We must transform this system. I applaud Toni for having the courage to not only speak out, but to eloquently document her story and findings. She is not alone; I have heard hundreds of parents speak with the same voice. I see this anguish on a daily basis in my work with adopted children.

Joyce Sterkel, Director, The Ranch for Kids, Eureka, MT

Second Time Foster Child is an outstanding book. It chronicles a horror story created by indifferent bureaucrats, ensconced in governmental silos, whose attitudes range from "we've always done it that way," to protecting their jobs, which often ignore the law or make their own where there is none. *Second Time Foster Child* should be read by everyone who works for or with a governmental child welfare agency, an adoption agency, or a juvenile court, as well as every state legislator and anyone who cares for the welfare of children. The situation described in this book has gone on far too long and must be fixed immediately.

Hugh Brady, President, NAMI Illinois

Second Time Foster Child is a must read for anyone claiming to support children and families in America. As clearly documented by Ms. Hoy, good hearts and intentions do not always lead to favorable results. The single track training by state agencies has led to an army of employees who can only see parents as abusive, neglectful monsters. This book brought uncontrollable tears. As an advocate for nearly forty years, my heart breaks that despite the presence and relentless work of groups like NAMI, many states are still destroying families in the name of treatment. It is hard to comprehend how any state thinks removing a loving family and natural supports from a child's treatment team (yet alone life) will somehow lead to treatment success. The state has a responsibility, over and above the process of adoption, to ensure the child and family has every opportunity to succeed. The emotional and financial consequences of failing to support the families the states help create cannot be ignored. *Second Time Foster Child* should send chills down every reader's spine because every parent/family is at risk for this type of abusive treatment from their state. Toni's brutal truth may not be welcome by those who like status quo, but I believe will be the country's best chance at opening a meaningful dialogue about the abusive practices and what truly needs to be done to preserve the forever families we have tried to create for these amazing, resilient children.

Sherry Howard-Wilhelmi, Chair of Arizona Governor's
Advisory Council on Developmental Disabilities,
Member of Arizona Human Rights Commission,
Member of Arizona Consortium for
Children with Chronic Illness Board

SECOND TIME FOSTER CHILD

*One Family's Fight
for Their Son's
Mental Healthcare
and Preservation
of their Family*

TONI HOY

NEW YORK

SECOND TIME FOSTER CHILD
One Family's Fight for Their Son's Mental Healthcare and Preservation of their Family

by TONI HOY

ISBN 978-1-61448-160-7 Paperback
ISBN 978-1-61448-161-4 EPub
Library of Congress Control Number: 2012930518

Published by:
Morgan James Publishing
The Entrepreneurial Publisher
5 Penn Plaza, 23rd Floor
New York City, New York 10001
(212) 655-5470 Office
(516) 908-4496 Fax
www.MorganJamesPublishing.com

Cover illustrated by:
Topper Helmers
topper14@aol.com

Cover Design by:
Rachel Lopez
www.r2cdesign.com

Interior Design by:
Bonnie Bushman
bbushman@bresnan.net

In an effort to support local communities, raise awareness and funds, Morgan James Publishing donates a percent of all book sales for the life of each book to Habitat for Humanity Peninsula and Greater Williamsburg.
Get involved today, visit
www.HelpHabitatForHumanity.org.

To Jim, Samantha, Mason, Katy, Chip, Daniel, Riley, and Randie

Face the sun, but turn your back to the storm.
Irish proverb

Thanks for weathering it with me.

PREFACE

RURAL LIVING DOESN'T OFTEN give rise to parallel parking, which is probably why I'm not very good at it. My husband always says, "Accelerate without fear." I approached writing "Second Time Foster Child" in much the same manner. I took some risks in writing this book. I took the risk of telling the truth about the tragedy of children who lost the love and support of their families, for a chance at getting well. I took the risk of exposing bad practice in state and local governments and other organizations. I portray the real horror that good parents face as they are criminalized trying to keep their families safe, while providing treatment for their mentally ill children. I also took some risks in divulging what transpired outside the court room and in closed-door meetings. I wrote this book with my audience in mind, fully aware that some of what I wrote would not be popular.

Chapter 18 speaks to the issue of how people become desensitized to a morally corrupt idea. People would be outraged that the government would forcibly take a child with cancer away from grieving parents in exchange for treatment, yet nonchalantly look the other way when the government takes a mentally ill child for the very same reason. When the Jews were liberated and the slaves were freed, the horrors of the captives were revealed, while the perpetrators were shamed. The overseers assigned to us were desensitized, dismissing our feelings of persecution. Sadly, those who seek to gain the most from this book will be the least likely to read it or to read it without making systemic excuses. It would have been easy for me to moderate the accounts to deemphasize the negative impact towards children and families.

Had I made that choice, the events that oppress families into making an unthinkable choice would once again be swept under the carpet, as they have for decades.

"Custody relinquishment for mental healthcare" is a term that governments and other organizations coined as a means for deeming the process acceptable. It's really a euphemism for *trading away custody rights.* Custody relinquishment sounds less abrasive, more tolerable, even crossing over to ordinary and customary. How different is it from the propaganda of the Holocaust or the pro-slavery movement? It was into the second year of our ordeal that I began regularly substituting a more fitting phrase. In public arenas, replacing the term "custody relinquishment" with "trading custody rights" caused visible discomfort.

"Second Time Foster Child" paints a picture of a narrow issue with a broad stroke, giving scope to a circumstance. Others have written about various child welfare laws or various aspects of laws. By forming a timeline of the laws, readers can see what is and what has been, as well as what can be. When the pieces are all in place, stark gaps and hard truths become evident, if not glaring.

This book is *my* story from *my* perspective. It holds *my* thoughts and *my* opinions. While it largely speaks to the effects of the system as they relate to fostering and adopting, the message transcends across other types of adoption, especially international adoptions in which there are high percentages of RAD (reactive attachment disorder) and FASD (fetal alcohol spectrum disorder), placing those children at high risk of adoption dissolution. Biological families are also at risk. While my book speaks specifically to issues relative to the state of Illinois, the basic concepts mirror problems that children and families face in many other states. It is my fervent hope that this book will cause other state systems to critically examine their own systemic gaps in order to better assist the families they serve.

My primary goal in writing this book is to increase awareness of the tragedy of involuntary relinquishment for mental healthcare. When I authored a short video called "He's My Son," I got emails from all over the country. They all said the same thing. "He's *My* Son" and "She's *My* Daughter" filled the subject line. The body of the emails spoke different words, but they all held the same meanings. People wrote that they could swap their family photos for ours and their child's photo for our child's photo. It was the same event with different faces. I wrote this book for the parents who lost custody of their children during the decades before us and who tried, but failed to get this barbaric practice stopped. I wrote it for parents presently caught in the shackles of injustice. I wrote it for families to come, that they would not suffer as we have. I wrote it to preserve history in the same way that photos were taken after the Holocaust, and that one day, custody relinquishment for mental healthcare will be abolished in every state. And I wrote it for my family.

All the names were changed to protect the innocent as well as those who made things unnecessarily difficult for us. The names of our immediate family members were not changed; nor was the name of our friend and attorney, Randie, for without whose kindness, compassion, wisdom, and support, I would never have endured this tragedy.

In living this ordeal, I have learned more about the system than I ever cared to know. Change is painstakingly slow, synergy is almost non-existent, and it all really comes down to one thing—*money*.

My secondary goal is to sound our voice to the professionals including state departments, judges, attorneys and other court related professionals, and clinicians. Along the beaten path, we encountered many professionals who were afraid to step out of their comfort zones, ignored the rules they were given, or in some instances, were just plain lazy. I give respect to the select few who ventured out on a limb on our behalf, faced criticism by their superiors as a result, and drew their own professional boundaries as to what degree they were willing to be part of such a broken system.

To the professionals in the child welfare and juvenile justice systems, I challenge each of you to ask yourselves the hard questions, as they pertain to your individual professions. If your goal is permanency, is it really permanent, or is it fluid? If you are seeking reunification, was it necessary to disband it to begin with? Are you treating the situation based upon its own merits? How willing are you to express to your superiors regarding the parts of your job that unnecessarily degrade and criminalize children and parents in exchange for mental healthcare? Are you coloring a clinical case as an abuse case? Are you doing the usual thing or the right thing? We drew the line at safety. Where do you draw it?

The fiber of this book revolves around two important words; permanency and oppression. Dissolution of the former, results in the latter. The predominant message of this book is that parents should never have to trade parental rights, to heal a child from any kind of brain disorder.

I challenge you to do as I have done. Accelerate without fear.

There were days that I just wanted to throw in the towel and give up. Regardless of how brutal it's been, I've been able to endure it all with full capability to regulate any of my emotions on any given day; sadness, frustration, anxiety, mistrust, anger, and even happiness. I wrote this book for my son, Daniel, who through no fault of his own, struggles with regulating every emotion, every day. On my worst day, it's still easier to be me.

> *In the depth of winter, I finally learned that within me, there lay an invincible summer.*
>
> Albert Camus

ACKNOWLEDGEMENTS

IN 2003 AND AGAIN IN 2005, devastated families across the nation approached their congressmen asking for a new law that would prevent involuntary relinquishment for mental healthcare. Their hopes were dashed when the Keeping Families Together Act failed to pass Congress in two consecutive congressional sessions. I wish to acknowledge the efforts of those families, who pioneered the path before us. I also acknowledge their sense of loss and emotional pain, as well as the pain for those who currently remain "in the trench."

I started writing my blog, Scope and Circumstance, as a resource for parents, never anticipating how popular it would become. I acknowledge my readership and blog-stalkers, many of which found my site in the wee hours of the night, over sleepless worry, and whose return trips make me realize the importance of keeping this media alive.

There is a lot to be said for timing. The Association for Community Mental Health Authorities in Illinois was looking for a parent advocate to aid their efforts in expanding the EPSDT provision of Medicaid. They found me. I applaud their efforts to expand EPSDT towards increasing availability of in-home and community based services, as well as the smaller contingency of folks like us, who actively sought critically needed residential care. I appreciate their concentrated efforts to make services available for families, especially Dee Ann Ryan, Executive Director, Vermilion County Mental Health Board, who like me, continues to lose sleep over families who cannot access mental healthcare.

The Community and Residential Services Authority, in Illinois, took notice of all the referrals I sent their way, helping many of the families "out of the trench." The Executive Director, John Schornagel, was my "Devil's advocate." Using his years of experience and expertise, he was an eager sounding board, always telling me why my ideas wouldn't work. These conversations helped me fine tune my advocacy work, giving it solid direction.

Words on a page cannot express the lifeline that our juvenile court attorney, Randie Bruno, has given us. She's been my rock and my right hand. She knew when to back me up, when to shut me up, and when to take the lead away from me completely. From her, I learned how to read the law. She was never afraid to offer the dark side of an issue in order to address any objections and to protect our interests. We held healthy and sometimes heated debates, but she was never afraid to call me on the carpet, nor to admit when she was wrong. If anyone gave me scope regarding the judicial system; it was Randie. I'd show up for court a stressed out mess. She'd show up smiling, and have me at ease in seconds flat. Her years of expertise and professionalism guided us down the murky path. We couldn't have held a better card in our deck.

The Collins Law firm gave us our lives back. Attorney, Aaron Rapier, took time to listen and soaked up the masses of information I gave him. He developed a solid game plan for success. Ours was more than a federal court case to him. We never doubted that he truly cared about our son and our family. Shawn Collins also believed in us, as well as in other adoptive families, current and future, who would be helped by their vital assistance.

I want to acknowledge the attorneys, who help us "trench-mongers" when all other efforts fail: Michelle Schneiderheinze, Robert Farley, John Lewis, Stephanie Altman, Janet Cartwright, Jane Perkins, Darcy Gruttadaro, Chris Koyanagi, and others whom I don't even know. I also acknowledge the work and career of Diane Redleaf and the Family Defense Center, who defends families against false allegations of abuse and neglect, as well as encourages me to continue "making noise" for family victims of false allegations involving mental health issues. For all the attorneys, their passion for helping families changes lives immeasurably. So many people would still be stuck "in the trench" without their valuable expertise and assistance. Future families will not endure emotional pain and financial hardship because of their professional efforts to aid and save families.

For Gail Krachtus, who has a book and story of her own, I appreciate her willingness to carve time out to meet with me to teach me about the authoring and publishing processes. Her advice and consult was invaluable. My editors and proofreaders, Robin Gerner, Kris Horn, and NAMI Illinois President, Hugh Brady, whose expertise and suggestions improved my book substantively; I acknowledge the gift of your valuable time, as well as your interest and support for my book's completion.

To acknowledge the people who helped us in the trench, especially "Ronald and Dr. Lisa" and a special thanks to Gregg Guentz, who gave us a much appreciated three hours of respite each week.

Free-lance artist, Topper Helmers, has done extensive work in the entertainment industry for Marvel Comics, Universal Studios, Disney Imagineering, and much more, as well as the design for the Lincoln Presidential Library and Museum, in Springfield, IL. I credit him with the genius behind the cover design, but more importantly, for personally encouraging our son, Daniel, to pursue his artistic talents, despite having a severe emotional disability.

I acknowledge my fellow advocates and system synergists, Michael Groomer and Beverly Hansen, from Advocates for Children of Trauma in Texas; Mary Thunker and Jen Genzler from Alphabet Soup Kids in Nebraska; the Michigan adoptive families, who filed suit against their state; Laurie Jarvis from Minnesota; and Marcia Stein from California, who continue the fight in their respective states. All have used my video, "He's My Son," as an advocacy tool, to educate others regarding the barbaric practice of trading custody rights for mental healthcare. Each, in his own way, continues to make a positive difference.

The NAMI Barrington Area Board of Directors and other NAMI members are the most active advocates I have the pleasure to know. They truly embrace the spirit of unconditional support and acceptance. I acknowledge their efforts to pull our family into their flock when everyone else cast us aside. Their passion to educate others, bust stigma, build supportive housing for the mentally ill, expand and increase mental health courts, and keep pressure on our state officials to support and keep mental health funding, gives voice to families who are too stressed to advocate for themselves. I look forward to a long and healthy partnership with all of you. In the coming years, we will accomplish many great things together. Thanks to you, I am proud to be a NAMI Mommy.

I duly note my family, who never minded that I was glued to my computer and encouraged me to speak out. Taking our story public was a full family decision. I appreciate your willingness to expose the details our lives to bring awareness to the stigma regarding mental health, and the tragedy of trading custody rights for mental healthcare, that other families may not suffer as we have.

TABLE OF CONTENTS

FOREWORD

Karl W. Dennis
President, Karl W. Dennis & Associates
Former Executive Director of Kaleidoscope, Inc., Chicago, IL
Making a Difference Award, 1995, Federation of Families
Marion F. Langer Award, American Orthopsychiatric Association
Life Time Achievement Award, International Conference on WrapAround Services
President's 1000 Points of Light Award, Points of Light Institute
National Honors Award, Annie E. Casey Foundation
National Award for Advocacy on Behalf of Children and Famlies, American Association of Community Psychiatrists

YEARS AGO WHEN I WAS learning how to best serve children and families; I discovered that parents were some of the very best teachers. I consulted them when I was stumped about a law – they would tell me the page and verse. I consulted them when I was stumped about educational services – they always knew who to talk to and what the law said. I also found that if I truly listened, the experiences they shared with me about their families, would always point in the direction services should take. Families have always been my teachers.

This is doubly true of Toni. Her story gives us the clues as to how services should be delivered. Toni and her husband adopted two sons, both with very special needs. Their journey speaks for the need for intensive in-home services, and the need to provide services that are family focused and driven, not child centered. Their journey also speaks to the need to be aware of and respond to the strain children with special needs put on siblings and other family members. This book reminds me that the richest of us, the poorest of us, and the wisest of us, still struggle to find appropriate services for their families from our current systems of care.

I am also reminded of a play I attended several years ago. An actor asked the audience, "What would they rather be, a flower or a weed?" Naturally most of the audience members raised their hands for being a flower. The actor then said that she would rather be a weed, as they have the traits of strength, persistence, and tenacity. And some of them are quite beautiful. I believe that you will agree that Toni and her family are definitely weeds. Weeds that struggle to survive; weeds that are persistent in their quest for appropriate services; and, weeds that are tenacious in their unconditional care for their children.

As I read this book, I continually asked myself which chapter was my favorite and my answer is always the same; they all were. I know you will feel the same.

In this book, you will not only hear of the Hoy's family struggle, but you will find a roadmap for how to navigate through the bureaucracy of laws, regulations, organizations, and roadblocks to services.

The book will lead you through our systems; their strengths, services, and their weaknesses. You will go away understanding the meaning of all those acronyms that we nod our heads in recognition of, but so often don't have a clue as to their meanings.

This is the best service primer I have ever read. It should be required reading for all service providers, human service workers, foster and biological parents, and politicians.

There is one caveat to the Hoy's family story, especially for service providers who read this book. The Hoy family reminds me of the great baseball player, Jackie Robinson. When the Brooklyn Dodgers first brought an African American player into the major leagues, they found Jackie Robinson, who was articulate, incredibly skilled, and had the ability to be loved by the fans. As other African American players came into the league, many people had expectations that they would be just like Jackie. We will do a great disservice to the families and youth we are privileged to serve, if we expect them all to be like the Hoy's. Families must be served without judgment. Some will be weeds, as Toni and her family are, and others will be like flowers. They all deserve our unconditional commitment.

I am in awe with how important this book is to the field. But I am equally in awe of this family, their love, persistence, and unconditional care they have given to each other. In the end it may be what pulls them through to a hoped for and successful conclusion.

FOREWORD

Dr. Ronald S. Federici, Psy.D, ABPN, ABMP, FPPR
Board-Certified Neuropsychologist
International Expert in International Adoption Medicine
Care for Children International, Inc.
Clinical-Developmental Neuropsychologist
Diplomate-American Board of Professional Neuropsychology (ABPN)
Diplomate-American Board of Medical Psychotherapists (ABMP)
Fellow in Advanced Clinical Psychopharmacology (FACAAP)
Fellow-American College of Professional Neuropsychology
Senior Fellow-National Academy of Neuropsychology
Diplomate-American Board of Disability Analysts (ABDA)
Diplomate-American Board of Cognitive-Behavioral Therapists
Father of Seven Internationally Adopted Children

THIS MOST POIGNANT BOOK highlights my thirty years of experience working with some of the most abused, neglected, and traumatized children, who have experienced profound deprivation, in various institutional care programs around the world. Mental health therapists and professionals alike, in addition to state and government officials, do not understand the severity and complexity of the traumatic effects of institutional care on children's brain growth and development, or the profound "neural developmental and psychological delays" which may later lead to maladaptive social and behavioral patterns within families.

The critical bonding and attachment period for traumatized, adoptive children has been significantly "disrupted," based on a modicum of high-risk, pre and postnatal factors including: institutional care, post-trauma, and immersion into a new family system following adoption, in which "adaptation" is yet another "foreign language." The majority of families I have encountered in my years of experiences and travels abroad, have been totally and unequivocally unprepared for the circumstances they find themselves in. The apathy and indifference of school officials, mental health professionals and many "critics" who have never treated, raised or worked in an institutional setting, makes the recovery for these children even more difficult.

Support for families who have very traumatized children is very minimal and many families are left feeling "unsupported." Social service agencies, schools, and even mental health professionals tend to look at this as a "family problem," as opposed to seeing the profoundly damaged children, who have literally survived the most traumatic levels of abuse and neglect. This truly makes these children victims of post-traumatic stress and they are faced with feelings of: "abandonment, depression, and loss of self."

Unfortunately, children coming out of traumatic backgrounds will display a wide variety of behavioral and very odd and unusual circumstances. Symptoms include; quasi-autistic patterns, various levels of acting out and defiance, as well as general noncompliance with treatment. In fact, these are all direct byproducts of debilitating anxieties; which include uncertainties and fears in establishing bonds or attachments with their new families. The traumatized children's initial "imprint" of safety and security has been fragmented, during early formative years. This combines with unspecified high risks, as well as pre and postnatal factors and neural genetic factors, which include the pervasive developmental patterns of trauma. Children who are adopted present with a very unique and complex set of challenges, in which our current social service, educational, and even medical communities struggle to understand. A huge "denial" exists which leads many to believe that internationally adopted and traumatized children are "no different" than U.S. foster care children. Hence, no special programs are designed to address the well-researched issues.

While there has been a new movement in the American Academy of Pediatrics Section on Adoption Medicine, in which to provide a better "medical model" of understanding adopted and traumatized children; there is still a paucity of information passed along in new professional's training. There aren't adequate specialized treatment providers and programs to perform proper evaluations along with intensive "reconstructive and developmental re-tracking" family therapies, in order to work with children and families, to heal the wounds, which are longstanding in nature.

The profound courage of the children who have survived institutional care and trauma, as well as the boldness and tenacity of families such as Toni Hoy's, and thousands of others I have worked with across the world, speaks to the fact that these children need well-informed and strong families to actually educate and remediate our current mental health and educational systems.

These are the same systems that tend to categorize these children as "no different than any other child who may have some learning or behavioral issues."

In my book entitled, "Help for the Hopeless Child: A Guide for Families," (with special discussion for assessing and treating the post-institutionalized child), I have outlined a proper program for neurodevelopmental and neuropsychiatric interventions. My upcoming book entitled "Escape from Despair: Through the Eyes of The Child," is written completely by the children who have survived trauma. The children's individual accounts relay some of the most painful, yet intense and factual accounts of how children themselves perceive their institutional care, lives, and environment, as well as their struggles in adapting to a new family.

A child's "new family" is not always the salvation most people and professionals may think it is. Often, nearly everything is totally alien to his/her thought process. This produces anxious-attachment patterns, which may intensify an ongoing struggle to find a way to "fit in" and become whole, after periods of profound neglect and deprivation. Bottom line: Love and rescue does not cure all time understanding, and reconstruction of a "damaged self," within the confines of a "new-safe reality," to achieve success.

Toni Hoy and many others like her are to be commended for never accepting a child as being "untreatable," and for also taking on a very archaic and poorly informed system of educators and professionals. These educators and professionals need to actually spend time in institutional/orphanage care and spend even more time reviewing the damaging effects of bonding-attachment "interruptions," which may lead to behavioral and social manifestations later. Post-traumatic stress and debilitating anxiety are the principal diagnoses, as opposed to the tons of diagnostic categories and medications many of these children are given.

There is NO shortcut in trauma therapy.

> *"If societies are judged by how they treat their most disabled members. Our society will be judged harshly indeed."*
>
> E. Fuller Torrey M.D.

Chapter One

AN AUTOBIOGRAPHICAL PERSPECTIVE

ON JULY 20, 2010, I sat in the Governor's office explaining how children, adopted out of foster care, were cycling back into the system. There is a gaping hole in the state mental healthcare system and our adoptive son fell into it. He became violent and aggressive due to pre-adoptive trauma. The state refused all sources of possible funding for the residential care he needed to keep himself and the rest of our family safe. The policy advisor responded with a question that I never saw coming.

"Why did you adopt those mentally ill kids anyway?"

I had to ransack my brain to find an adjective to describe the way that question made me feel. The only one I could think of was a word that is used often in England, but rarely here.

Gobsmacked!

I took a moment to compose myself before I responded, "Because I'm darn good at it! Because not just anyone can love a mentally ill child—I can. The state of Illinois needs people like me."

I still wonder just exactly where this policy advisor thought mentally ill children should be. As parents of two mentally ill children, we have experienced a lot of stigma, but I certainly didn't expect to get it from the most senior health policy advisor in the state. Once I got over the shock; I realized it was really a two part question. Why did we adopt? Why did we choose to raise mentally ill children?

Why We Adopted

I'll explain why we chose adoption versus giving birth first. We had physical and emotional reasons for choosing adoption. There are a lot of things in life I do very well. Physically speaking, pregnancy and childbirth are not included among those things. Our emotional reasons for considering adoption stem back to my husband's and my own childhoods.

We are not an infertile couple. I gave birth to two of the most beautiful red-headed children you've ever seen. In fact, when we disclosed to our families that we intended to adopt, one of my sisters-in-law asked, "Why would you want to do that? You have the prettiest babies in the family." I believe that my nieces and nephews are all beautiful in their own way, but I suppose there is something especially engaging about a porcelain skinned baby with the perfect shade of amber curls. In fact, strangers have long stopped us on the streets to ask us if our daughter's hair was real or a wig. So, what was to stop us from having another equally beautiful child?

The issue of getting pregnant was not an obstacle for my husband, Jim, and me. In fact, in that realm, my biological clock never skipped a beat. We chose to have children and weeks later, I was pregnant. No waiting or wondering required. But, the issues of pregnancy and childbirth were entirely another matter. Just weeks after becoming pregnant, if I could make it from the bed to the bathroom before the morning sickness hit; it was a good day. None of the remedies, old or new worked. I was miserable for five to six months. About the time I could actually keep a meal down, I was so uncomfortably large, I could barely move around. I stand five feet nothing with a very short torso, so there was really no room for a baby to grow. Once it did grow, there was no space left for my bladder. After suffering a miserable miscarriage following my first pregnancy, I decided

I'd had enough of hospitals. A co-worker had been telling me about how wonderful home birth was. After researching the differences thoroughly, it sounded like the most comfortable option for me. What I didn't anticipate was having a December baby in the Midwest, when it was 30 degrees below zero and having a virus with a fever at the time I went into labor. This precluded me from having the uneventful home birth I desired and sent me off to the hospital with a broken water bag and water freezing as it ran down my legs.

In 1989, my first full term pregnancy yielded the first of our two red headed cherubs, but not before 24 hours of hard labor followed by a Cesarean section birth. Five days after I came home from the hospital, we celebrated Christmas with our daughter, Samantha.

In 1991, my next pregnancy was identical to the last, except that two weeks after my due date, I was still pregnant. I was beyond uncomfortable and barely walking the week before I gave birth. Apparently, my body does not dilate, so once again, I was under the knife with an unplanned Cesarean section. The second incision was cut longer due to the size of our first born son, Mason, who weighed in at almost 11 lb., and stretched the measuring tape to 24 inches. We brought him home from the hospital in clothing for a 6–9 month old. He was three feet shorter than me at birth and my small frame didn't manage the experience very well. It stands to reason, that a large baby gets even bigger after he's born. It was not long at all before he was too heavy for me to carry him around. To make matters worse, I herniated a disc in my back, requiring surgery. When our pudgy little tyke could finally crawl, I taught him to wait until I sat down, and coaxed him to crawl onto my lap, so that I could hold him.

After our second baby, I started to re-think the plan about having a third child, but my husband very much wanted another one. We wondered if my back would support another pregnancy, and then, there was the issue of carrying the infant post birth. While another birth was physically possible, it wasn't really plausible, especially with already having two little ones at home. Ultimately, we decided another birth from my body was out of the question.

In 1994, a baby boy was born in another part of our county. He was starved, lethargic, and severely neglected. After being admitted to the hospital, he was diagnosed with "failure to thrive." The nurses fed him with an eyedropper once an hour to keep him alive. He almost died. Social services removed his older brother and sister from that same home a few weeks later. Their sister was placed with one of her birth father's biological relatives, who declined to take in her brothers. The boys initially went to live with their birthmother's parents and later to a foster home. They'd been in foster care nearly two years when we, a family living not too far away, began to think about adoption.

Around the time my soon-to-be adopted son was turning two years old, I found myself thinking, "If I could just give birth to a two year old." That, I thought to myself, I could manage. And then I thought, why couldn't we bring another child into our family at the age of two? Adoptable children were available in every age. Certainly, there was a parentless two-year-old out there somewhere, who needed a mommy and daddy to love him.

My husband had his own reasons for wanting to adopt. He'd had a childhood friend who suffered through a horrible foster family experience. He would never forget times spent with his good friend as they were growing up. They enjoyed time together and spent a lot of time talking about sports, life, love, and family. My husband felt a pang of guilt that he'd been raised in such a large, loving, close family, while his friend lived in a home where he was treated like a second class citizen. His friend felt overworked and under-appreciated. He hadn't felt loved or a vital part of his foster family. My husband felt sure that he could make a foster experience much better for any children that we might bring into our family. When discussing such issues as race or age, Jim didn't even have a preference. We did agree on one thing. We weren't in a hurry to adopt. Because we already had two children, we were far more concerned that any children that might come to live with us, had to fit well into our family dynamics. We would rather wait a longer time to find just the right match. I hadn't known any foster children as I grew up, but I could have been one myself; so I knew how important fitting into a family could be.

I was the third of five children and the oldest girl. My mother was only 20 years old when I was born. I suppose she would have been described at that time as a blonde bombshell. She was gorgeous. However, to the same degree that she was outwardly beautiful, she was inwardly manic. Men swooned over her and when I was very small, as rumor would have it, she had a few trysts with other men. My parents separated a few times during my early childhood. When I was ten years old, I heard rumblings that our mother was having an affair with our father's best friend. Being young, I wasn't quite sure what to believe. Then my mother disappeared. She left a note saying that she could no longer deal with being a mother and had to leave for her own sanity. Everyone drew their own conclusions when she returned, many months later, with our dad's best friend. It was during her absence that I nearly became a foster child. My dad, barely 30 years old, didn't feel capable of raising a 2 year old, a 5 year old, and three more kids aged 10, 11, and 12. He considered placing all of us in foster care, but was talked out of it by caring friends and relatives who offered to help him. The courts ultimately sent my younger sisters to live with our mother, who was often demanding and unstable, screaming and acting irrational. She began drinking excessively, which increased her mania.

My middle sister, five years younger than me, was always in trouble and ran away from home starting in her early teens. As an older teen and into her adult years, she abused drugs and alcohol and had all four of her kids taken from her by social services. My sister was ultimately diagnosed with bipolar disorder. She has since completed alcohol rehabilitation and is stable on medicine. She has been successful in marriage and work for many years now. The outcome for our mother was not as successful.

Mom continued to self-medicate with alcohol and prescription drugs. She was never formally diagnosed or treated, but the signs of bipolar disorder were clear. Her mania escalated to the degree that she was not able to have a relationship with anyone. She became a total recluse of her own choosing. She died alone, as she lay in a filthy slum for two days before anyone discovered her. When she died, we didn't even know where she was. While I hadn't lived with my mother or my sister during my teen and young adult years, the mal-effect of their mental illnesses affected my life in too many negative ways. It was for these reasons that we decided to draw a firm line against accepting children with mental illness. Little did we know that caseworkers were regularly placing small children, with frontal lobe brain damage, due to severe neglect, into adoptive homes. The caseworkers failed to use foresight to educate prospective adoptive parents about what trauma could look like years later, favoring to emphasize that things would "settle down in time."

Why We Adopted Mentally Ill Kids

The short answer to the second part of the policy advisor's question was that we didn't, in fact, want to adopt kids with mental illness. That was never part of a known choice. We were told that the worst of our two adoptive sons' problems was severe neglect and once they were adopted into a permanent, loving home, they'd be "just fine." Because of mental illness experiences within my own family, it was number one on our "no" criteria. While we resigned to take children that had mild physical disorders, mental health issues were off the table. It was the one area we didn't want to contend with. It had already made my life a living hell. The fact that our adoptive children had mental illness was not a known issue at the time they came to live with us. We weren't told and we weren't given enough history to figure it out. We just didn't know.

We did, however, have other decisions to make such as what type of adoption was right for us and what adoptive criteria would yield the perfect addition to our family. First, we researched the different paths to adoption.

Adoption Decisions

Finding a child from another country and proceeding with an international adoption was on the list of possibilities. Several countries were open to American adoptions. However, international adoption would require travel out of the country, which albeit exciting, was also the most expensive option. We didn't have tens of thousands of dollars. It was out of our budget. There was private adoption, which was almost equally as expensive. Waiting lists for private adoptions are very long and we didn't feel right about taking a placement when childless parents had been waiting years for their turn at parenting. We felt as though we'd be depriving an infertile couple of the joys of parenthood. Then I read about something I'd never heard about before, "legal risk" adoption.

We selected a local private agency that had an adoption department. The nuns who worked in foster care explained the process of "legal risk" adoption to us. This was a program in which kids came into pre-adoptive homes through foster care. Caseworkers matched foster children, who were unlikely to return to their parents, with licensed foster families interested in adopting. The child avoided multiple placements in foster care. The worker didn't have to constantly move him. The family got a chance to get acquainted with the child prior to adoption. This would provide some assurance that the placement would work out. When biological parental rights were severed, the child or children could be adopted by the family who had already been caring for them. It was less traumatic for the children this way–far less traumatic than placing children with one family not interested in adoption and then moving them to an adoptive home when the children became legally free for adoption. Legal risk adoption is considered a win-win situation for everyone.

Fostering children who were likely to become free for adoption looked like the perfect solution for us. In choosing this option, we had to come to terms with the fact that, while we may have wanted the children to stay with us, there was also a risk that the best option might be for them to return home. If that happened, we'd be expected to support the decision for them to return to their birth families. This was a risk we were willing to take.

The process in completing the application for "legal risk" adoptive-foster care was a bit more involved than we anticipated. We had to take classes, fill out forms, have physicals, arrange a home inspection, and even get fingerprinted. Our other children had to complete some of these tasks as well. Other than a positive tuberculosis skin test for me, which a chest X-ray revealed was inactive; we sailed through the rest with flying colors.

The next step was for us to do mini-autobiographies and tell them as much about ourselves as we could. Then we had to fill out a stack of paperwork which would help them piece together our family dynamics and work in conjunction with our hopes and dreams. This would help them select a child who was best suited to become a member of our family.

One of the most difficult stages was to identify the types of illnesses and disorders that we were willing to accept and thought we could manage.

Parents of biological children deal with whatever situations arise without thinking, because there is a biological connection and they love their children so much. Not loving a sick child isn't an option. Unlike biological connections, adoption gave us the chance to weed out the issues and conditions that scared us the most, and that we'd rather not have to deal with. I have to admit that it felt a bit liberating to have so much control. At the same time, we felt a bit uneasy about selecting a child in this manner. To some degree, it reeked of grabbing a bruised piece of produce and then putting it back on the shelf. It had an almost inhuman quality about it. At the same time, we didn't want to get in over our heads with issues we knew that were not equipped to handle. Little did we know that the control we were being given was completely illusory.

The nuns at the social service agency cautioned that if we didn't want to deal with problems, we should not continue the process. They warned us that all foster children came with a variety of different academic, behavioral, mental, and physical disorders, due to the trauma that they experienced within their birth families or within other foster families. We could expect traumatized children, but they also assured us that we'd be trained in caring for them appropriately. We had to learn about different types of abuse and how to deal with adoptive issues.

The social workers educated us about the kinds of reasons children came into foster care: neglect, physical abuse, sexual abuse, and prenatal substance abuse affect. They also counseled us about the importance of making a forever commitment to the children, emphasizing that disrupting or dissolving an adoption was a very painful experience for everyone involved. At the time, we didn't give these words of caution much credence, but they would come back to haunt us over ten years later. Many of the children we'd be asked to consider might have more than one type of abuse, possibly combined with neglect. We considered all of these very carefully and began to form an impression of the kinds of issues we thought we could manage. We also considered the potential impact these abuses might have towards our biological children.

Since neither of us had any prior experience with adoption, we surmised that the hardest part was going to be helping the children feel loved and accepted. Most of the children, available for adoption had been rejected by adult caregivers many times over. It would be our job to help them understand past relationships as well as help them resolve past hurts. We'd need to reassure them that temporary gave way to permanent and this home was the end of the line. Dealing with adoptive issues would not be a one-shot conversation. We would have to help them put their feelings about adoption in perspective throughout the rest of their lives. Besides deciding about physical, trauma, and adoptive issues, we also had to decide about the age and race of a child we were to bring into our home.

Because of my weak back, we requested to foster/adopt children who were old enough to walk, so that I would not have to carry them. Upon the advice of a sweet little old nun, we also requested that the ages of prospective adoptive children be limited to ages younger than our biological children. Since our youngest son was about five years old at the time, our options were fairly limited, to between the ages of two and four. When we got to the question regarding race, we were presented with a chart. Small, connecting square boxes stretched across the page horizontally. The box to the far left was white. The next box was a faint gray. The boxes got gradually darker moving along to the right. The end box was completely dark. There was a little circle beneath each box. We had to mark, on a scale from lightest to darkest, how dark skinned a child we would accept, should they decide to place an African American child in our home. We were completely stunned. It was the one part of that interview that I will never forget. They answered our expressions of surprise and disgust by saying that to some people, the degree of darkness did indeed, matter. We stuck to our original decision of requesting children who would fit well with our other kids and fit well into our family, regardless of race.

Navigating through the list of medical issues was much harder. Since we hadn't had any issues with our biological children to date, we weren't really certain what medical issues we could actually handle. We quickly weeded out some medical problems, consisting mostly of issues that were certain to be life-long conditions. We didn't desire to take care of intensive physical needs for the rest of our lives, although we greatly admire people who not only do it, but do it with joy. After all, we did have choices. We opted out of severe physical needs. Although checking off the lists of physical conditions were exceptionally difficult to complete, the mental health columns were a breeze. No, no, no, and no, some more. We weren't prepared for it and we knew we couldn't handle it. No thank you.

In February, 1998, we took the plunge and began our "Foster Pride Classes." We signed up for the Foster Pride Classes through the Department of Children and Family Services (DCFS). Taking the ten modules of Foster Pride classes in order to become formally licensed as foster parents netted an interesting set of revelations for me. Being an inherent geek, initially, I ate up the lessons. Then we had Session Four: Meeting Developmental Needs/Loss.

Meeting Developmental Needs/Loss is a module that deals with helping a child come to terms with feelings of separation and abandonment. Even when a child lives in an abusive environment, we were taught that he still has feelings of love and caring for his family members or caregivers. To be separated from them, even when it's necessary, is emotionally traumatizing for children, even when it is in their overall best interests. Session Four is designed to help parents pull out their own hurts and demons, analyze how they resolved them, and determine how they can use their past experiences to help children heal. This was the module that separated the women from the girls. This was the module that sent a lot of parents packing. *I was almost one of them.* Drudging up childhood experiences was pleasant for many. For others, it was like reliving a bad dream. As a child of a caustic, dysfunctional family, I began to feel inferior. I surmised that the Foster Pride instructors and the caseworkers were really looking for that perfect set of parents who were raised by yet another set of perfect parents.

About the same time, we had an unexpected development. Some troubled teens came into our lives. It quickly became clear to my husband, Jim, and me, that we had very different gifts to offer. We discovered my husband had the gifts of sympathy and compassion. I discovered I had the gift of identification. When it came to talking to the kids about their hurts and hardships, I could empathize and identify. I connected with them better in those moments while my husband sat feeling inept. Yet, during better times, he rose to the top, demonstrating that joy and happiness was attainable. Ultimately, we decided that we balanced each other out pretty well. It became clear that perhaps we were a good team to do this kind of work. I discovered even more about myself in a later module that helped me solidify my own commitment to fostering and adopting.

I vividly recall another class which forced me to do a little soul searching. We were instructed to write our name in the middle of a piece of paper and draw a circle around it. Surrounding our name, we each had to write all the components of our lives, including our family members, jobs, hobbies, friends, and activities. Then we each had to draw a line from each life component to the circle with our name inside of it. The type of line we drew indicated the type of relationship we had with that person or activity. A bold, straight line was a healthy relationship. A jagged line indicated a rocky relationship. A wavy line was a weak or distant relationship. A dashed line indicated a broken relationship. I completed the exercise and gave it scope. I had strong lines for nearly every circle, except the ones for my parents, which were broken lines. I learned a few things from this exercise. I learned that all of the relationships I had in my life were good ones, except for those with my parents. Since you cannot have a relationship with someone who doesn't want to have one with you, those relationships were out of my control. Mostly, what I learned about myself was that my life had good balance. Nothing heavily over-shadowed anything else. The instructor shared with us that his own chart made him realize that he worked too much and was quite boring. Since he worked as a clinician, I hadn't done bad, comparatively speaking.

Sometimes you learn as much from what goes wrong as you do from what goes right. I learned that I had become a good person in spite of my childhood. That settled it. My feelings of inadequacy dissipated. We were ready to become foster/adopt parents. I never regretted not dropping out of that class.

"I prayed for this child, and the
LORD has granted me what I asked
of him."

1 Samuel 1:27

Chapter Two

TWO BOYS AND THE IMPORTANCE OF PERMANENCY

I HAVE COME TO THE CONCLUSION that no matter how much you try to prepare to receive more children into your home, you're never completely ready. Nonetheless, we prepared by reading books and meeting together with other foster and adoptive parents. It was time well spent. We learned so much from others who were further down that road. It also helped us narrow in on what we could and couldn't handle. We wanted to hear everyone's stories of how they transitioned the kids into their homes and how they helped the kids adjust. The foster parents we know have a lot of compassionate and creative ideas for helping kids gain a sense of belonging. The common thread amongst them was to find a way to help them embrace their new families, while hanging onto some pieces of their biological families.

Throughout the Foster Pride classes, we felt a little outcast. All of the other families already had foster children placed under their care. We didn't. We listened attentively to stories about what it was really like to bring neglected and abused children into their homes.

One day, after class, we had lunch with a nun, who was the adoption supervisor at the adoptive agency that we'd selected. Between bites of her burger, she probed us about the type of child we thought would be the best case scenario for us. One of the questions she asked was, if we could choose the perfect age, which would we select? I answered quickly, "A two year old." As I recall, she dropped her burger onto the plate and stared at me with complete astonishment. "In my decades as an adoption supervisor, no one has ever asked me for a two year old! You can't be serious!" I was totally serious. It's my favorite age. I think two year olds are completely fascinating. A two year old is filled with curiosity, which is why they are always getting into things. But if you pay close attention, it's also the stage when the world around them finally begins to make sense. Every time they figure something out, their faces completely light up. It's like having a continuous "aha!" moment. Such pure joy is contagious! I love two year olds.

We could almost see the wheels turning inside her head. She now knew that I loved two year olds. I had mentioned in class that our other kids were redheads. She had an "aha!" moment of her own. She had a placement in mind for us. We asked to see a photo of the child. No, she would not show it to us. She recalled there was some reason this placement might not be right for us, but she'd check the files and get back to us. We asked if she had the photo with her. She smiled and said yes. Could we *puleez* see it? She smiled and politely said no, not until she was sure. Apparently, there was no sweet talking this nun. She promised to check things out and call us if she thought it was a fit.

The following week, the Sister called and asked if we'd consider not one, but two little boys. Now that was a curve ball! We'd been thinking that we'd make an entrance into the foster-adopt arena slowly, one child at a time. We hadn't thought beyond taking more than one child, at least not to begin with. Two boys? Did we have space for them? Did we want to jump in head first, with two boys? She told us a bit more about them. She'd thought about us because one of them had red hair, just like our other kids. He was three years old. His brother was an adorable blue-eyed blonde. She'd thought about us for him too, because he was two years old. They desired to keep the brothers together. She told us that they'd been neglected and they were looking for a pre-adoptive home for them. They were fairly certain the birth parents' rights would be severed by the court. The kids were small and they wanted to place them with a family who would be willing to adopt them if fate held that they remained wards of the state. They'd been in relative care for a year followed by another six months in foster care. The foster mother had advocated for an adoptive home for them in court. Prenatal substance abuse exposure was suspected, but not confirmed. They were certain that once these little guys were accepted into a loving adoptive family home, they'd be "just fine." It certainly seemed like a good fit. She finally showed us a photograph of them. They were completely adorable. They grabbed a piece of our hearts from the moment we set eyes on that photo.

About a week later, the sweet nun handed our case over to a case worker, who was assigned to our family. He was a large man, who was personable and friendly. He expressed genuine interest in getting to know us better. We could see that he was dedicated to making sure the boys were loved and cared for and that he wanted them to have a permanent home.

Generally, the first meeting between prospective parents and pre-adoptive children takes place at a neutral setting. We agreed to meet the boys for the first time at a fast food restaurant. We got there first and waited anxiously for them to arrive with their current foster mother. Our children, Samantha and Mason, were very excited. They were happy to be getting two new brothers. The caseworker introduced us to them. Daniel was a blue-eyed, blonde-haired cherub. He was my two year old. Chip was 18 months older, a blue-eyed redhead, who bore an uncanny resemblance to our biological children. No wonder the Sister had thought of us. We talked and played and held them on our laps. They were balls of energy, racing all over the place, and jibber-jabbering non-stop. It was difficult to visit or talk. The caseworker wanted to know our thoughts. He asked if we wanted to take time to think about it? "No," we replied, "they are perfect as any children could be. We'd love to have them come live with us." Once again, our new caseworker reminded us that "legal risk" foster care did not always result in adoption. If it was meant to be, we were certain it would happen. If not, it meant another child was out there waiting for us. We asked the boys what they would think about having us for a mom and dad. They nodded their head excitedly and exclaimed, "Yes!" And then Chip looked at Samantha and Mason and said, "Do we get the kids too?"

We answered through giggles, "Yes, you're going to have a new sister and brother." I held little Daniel in my lap and marveled at what a beautiful little boy he was. He was to become my son. Then he did something that he would do many times over in the weeks and months ahead that just melted my heart. He put his little hands on my cheeks and said, "You pretty Mom!" and kissed me on the lips.

A week later, we visited them at their foster family's home. We celebrated our new family together with their foster family. We ate pizza and ice cream. In another week's time, they came home for the first time, for the whole weekend. It was utter chaos and a complete blast. We had three twin beds lined up in a row in the boys' room. Stuffed animals flew across the room about half the night. We fell in love with the boys and couldn't wait for them to come home permanently. Two weeks after that, the foster mother arrived at our house with two boys in tow, and three small boxes of clothes and toys. It was all they had and most of it had come from the foster family. We had two additional Easter baskets ready and waiting for them.

A Sad Day and a Happy Day

April 14, 1995, was Good Friday. The boys moved into our home. They helped me put their clothes in the drawers and put their toys away. The next thing I did was to cuddle them up in my lap and read them a pre-school version of the Easter story. We focused on Good Friday. I told them that Good Friday was a happy day and a sad day. It was a sad day because Jesus died on the cross. It was a happy day because he died to pay for all of our sins. It was a sad day for another reason too. Today, Daniel and Chip had left their biological family behind, along with everything that was special and familiar to them. It was a happy day because they got a mom and a dad and a brother and a sister, a forever family. Permanency.

They were much too young to understand the significance of the story that day. We repeated the story annually and it became a part of their adoption story. Two days after I read it to them for the first time, we celebrated Easter. It was time for coloring eggs and visiting the Easter bunny. We had an Easter egg hunt in our house. It took them a while to catch on. Samantha and Mason passed over some eggs that were not so well hidden, to let the younger boys have a chance. Soon they caught on and found their fair share. We gave them their Easter baskets full of candy. Within minutes, and before we noticed, they had eaten every piece of it. Lesson number one in foster parenting; limit the amount of candy. They couldn't regulate it on their own. We got them dressed in their Sunday best and jubilantly drove to church to rejoice in the resurrection with our church family. We took two cars. It was time to buy a mini-van. The children needed us and we wanted them. Chip and Daniel were just two of the thousands of children in Illinois who got an adoptive home that year.

As the foster child population swelled during the nineties, adoption became a nationwide hot topic, one that was of particular interest to President William Clinton and First Lady Hillary Rodham Clinton.

The Adoptive and Safe Families Act of 1997

President Clinton signed the Adoptive and Safe Families Act on November 19, 1997, just three years and five days after Daniel was born. This Act is commonly known by its acronym, ASFA, and will be referred to as such throughout the remainder of this book. State social service agencies expressed increasing alarm, relative to the expanding number of children growing up in foster care. The main purpose of the law was to move the droves of children out of foster care and into permanent adoptive homes. How did so many children end up in foster care to begin with?

Let's give the issue scope. According to Cathleen S. Graham's scholarly journal called "Implementation of the Adoptive and Safe Families Act of 1997: The Indiana Experience," the number of foster children increased nationally by 74% from 1986 to 1995, swelling to 486,000. What societal changes precipitated this colossal increase?

The obvious answer partially has to do with the general increase in the number of overall births from the late 1960's through the 1980's. We attribute this increase to the "Baby Boomer" generation, which increased our nation's population en masse, during their child bearing years.

A large number of children who ended up in foster care were sired by parents during the 1970's and 1980's. Both decades were a time of significant, societal change for women. The 1960's gave way from the stay-at-home mother of the past, to the supermom of the future. Charles of the Ritz, a perfume company summed up the change succinctly with its 1980 commercial for its new perfume, Enjoli. "I can bring home the bacon, fry it up in a pan, and never, never let him forget he's a man, cuz I'm a woman, Enjoli!" as three images of the same woman danced around, appropriately donning a business suit, casualwear, and a cocktail dress. These images clearly depicted the new roles of the modern woman. Women were rising to the top. Billie Jean King made headlines when she defeated Bobby Riggs. Little League baseball and military academies began to accept girls into their formerly all-male worlds. Women began to preface their names with a new title, Ms., a happy medium between Mrs. and Miss. They took their new titles out of the home and into the workplace.

During these two decades, there were other significant societal changes taking place at the same time. The 70's was a time of peace and free love. Eighteen year olds received the right to vote. The drugs of choice were heroin and LSD. During the 80's LSD and heroin gave way to crack and cocaine as the more popular drugs of choice. Also, during the 1980's, the nation had a brand new concern and it was deadly-the AIDS epidemic. Those practicing free love either took sexual protection to a new level or risked exposure to the deadly virus. Adding increasing societal drug abuse and the AIDS epidemic to the rising baby boom, the foster rolls began to increase in rapid numbers.

Illegal drug use amongst child bearing women and men became an increasing problem. Drug treatment centers sprang up to treat addicted individuals whose lives had become unmanageable due to drug addiction. Concurrently, a collateral problem arose in the offspring population.

"Having Attention-Deficit/Hyperactivity Disorder and Substance Use Disorder: A Review of Literature," by Dominique Eich and Bernd Figner, of Zurich University Hospital, lists a conglomeration of studies which link prenatal heroin and cocaine use to attention-deficit/hyperactivity disorder, more commonly known as ADHD. Studies show that while the effects are not overtly noticeable during infancy and younger childhood, issues as hyperactivity, impulsivity, and emotional disregulation occur in increasing numbers during adolescence, and don't improve with the onset of adulthood. Worse, when ADHD results from prenatal drug use, even recreational drug use, prescription medications are not always effective. It should be no surprise that Generation Y of the 1990's yielded an influx of children with ADHD diagnoses.

With the induction of Generation Y, came a plethora of substance addicted mothers who were either abusing or neglecting their children. Some of the children died. This netted a foster care panic, which is detailed in Richard Wexler's "Take the Child and Run: Tales from the Age of ASFA." Wexler explains "foster care panics," detailing how children who died following multiple entrances into the foster care system, caused governments to take children away from their parents in alarming numbers. Social workers were instructed to "err on the side of the child" rather than use credible evidence based upon a thorough investigation, when deciding to remove a child from his parent's care. According to Wexler, it was the government's way of protecting itself from media criticism. However, his report also notes that the number of foster children was already increasing prior to the "crack epidemic." Foster care panics added to the number of children entering the system due to drug addicted parents and the AIDS epidemic. There were so many children in foster care during the 1990's, people began to question what was best for the large number of children who were growing up in foster care. ASFA mandated that parents, whose children remained in foster care for 15 of 22 months, would be subject to complete termination of parental rights. First lady, Hillary Rodham Clinton waged a movement to move children out of foster care and into adoptive homes. With presidential and congressional support, ASFA was passed in the 105th Congress.

ASFA offered financial incentives to state governments who were interested in decreasing their foster child populations and increasing their adoptive populations. States heavily recruited adoptive parents using strong adoption campaigns including media ads. President Clinton challenged states to double the number of adoptions within five years. Illinois met this goal the first year, under DCFS Director, Jess McDonald. In 2002, Illinois won 5 out of 18 adoption awards and 3 more in 2003, including one for a successful adoption recruiting program called, "One Church, One Child." The program encourages African American churches to recruit one adoptive family each year to adopt one waiting African American child. DCFS co-founded the program in Chicago. The adoption recruitment campaign was a success. According to Illinois DCFS records, Illinois boasted 7,275 finalized adoptions in 1999, a 294% increase over 1997.

Foster-adoptive parents like us, witnessed a new set of social services phraseology, which included:

"The birth parents must cooperate, comply with the terms of the service agreement, or risk termination of parental rights."

"The birth parents have one year to get their act together or they lose their children forever."

"The parents must correct the conditions which brought them into care."

"We don't want them languishing in foster care."

"We don't want them moving from foster home to foster home."

"Children deserve permanency."

Permanency. That was the buzz word of the time. I heard it over and over again. I heard it during every monthly caseworker visit; every administrative case review; every court hearing. Permanency. It was all about giving the child a permanent, "forever" family. As Generation Y moved closer to adolescence, a new trend emerged that threatened the notion of permanency and thrust a financial burden on the states that they were not prepared to handle. (I save the rest of the discussion surrounding ASFA for Chapter 13, where the promise of a "forever" family for Daniel, under the law, is discussed in light of his and our family's journey.)

On May 18, 1998, in Waukegan, Illinois, a circuit court judge tapped her star-tipped wand onto the heads of me, my husband, our biological children, Samantha and Mason, and our newly adopted boys, Chip and Daniel, making us a permanent, forever family.

Permanency. They told all of us it was *permanent.*

Chapter Three

DIAGNOSING TRAUMA AND MENTAL ILLNESS IN CHIP

DOUBLING THE NUMBERS OF children in our family was an initial adjustment. In time, we developed routines. Overall, we were quite pleased with our new family. Problems surfaced, as we anticipated they would, but we felt confident that we could tackle anything that came our way. Each boy brought his own unique set of problems, most of which weren't the types of problems that we expected. Through trial and error, we learned a lot about which approaches worked, as well as the ones that didn't. And eventually, our journey took us to a place, that in our wildest dreams, we never anticipated.

So, what is it *really* like raising foster children? They didn't sit under furniture and rock to soothe themselves like other foster parents told us they might. Our training paid off in some areas, but there were others that baffled us completely.

We immediately noticed effects of starvation. Most notably, both boys' skin had a yellowish cast to it. Daniel was fair and blonde, but tanned easily in the summer. His skin had a sallow hue to it. Chip was a redhead. Already having two redheads, as well as having extended family members with red

20

hair, we knew what his skin should look like. Redheads had pale skin with a pinkish cast to it. Chip looked a little orange. When he was mad, his little red eyebrows turned bright orange. The palms of his hands and the bottoms of his feet also had an orangey cast to them. We noticed other signs of starvation as well.

Both boys got up in the wee hours of the morning to scrounge for food. Every day for years, I woke up bleary eyed in a race to beat them to the kitchen where I'd tell them, "In our house, Mommy makes breakfast and there will always be some for you to eat." They stole food from everywhere, the refrigerator, the cabinets, other people's plates, and the garbage. We had to put some food items on top of the kitchen cabinets so they couldn't reach them. I had to alter my way of serving food. Before they came to live with us, I'd set the table and then serve each plate with each food item. I soon discovered this was not a good process for the boys. If I put hot food on their plates, they stuck their hands right in it and burned their hands. If I put fruit on their plates, Chip would eat all of it and ask for more before I got any food at all on anyone else's plate. I had to serve the food and then bring the plates to the table, making sure the food wasn't too hot. Soon, they learned to wait until after prayers before digging in. Chip could not seem to get enough fruit. No matter how much fruit we gave him, he always wanted more. Neither of them wanted to eat meat. It was too much work for them to cut it and chew it. They ate very fast and chewed very little, swallowing large amounts of it whole. Daniel would stuff his little cheeks so full of food, he couldn't chew at all and had to spit it back out onto the plate. Though we coached them to slow down and chew more thoroughly while eating meals, it was one area that we were never completely successful. At times, their lust for food caused us concern for their safety.

A few months after the boys came to live with us, it was summer. We attended barbecues and picnics. It was difficult to keep tabs on them. With so many people around them, it was easy for them to be sneaky, stealing food, and wandering off. They'd take food off other guest's plates and eat it right in front of them. They'd take leftover food from the garbage and eat it. They'd grab handfuls of cookies and cake, eating large amounts of both. They'd drink anything that was in a can, including beer. We found we weren't able to enjoy ourselves, having to watch them so closely. One day, I had all the kids in the car and I needed to run into the house for one minute. I grabbed the mail and set it on the seat. I returned to find my 7 year old daughter in a complete panic. Chip had grabbed a sample packet of bright yellow liquid floor cleaner. My daughter snatched it from him before he ripped it open to drink it, shouting at him, "That's not juice! Mom cleans the floor with that stuff! It will kill you!" We began to be afraid that one of them would accidentally ingest something lethal. But dealing with food issues was not nearly as bad as dealing with the tantrums.

Both boys screamed a lot. It was not just a run of the mill scream. It was the blood curdling, gut wrenching, clap-your-hands-over-your-ears kind of screaming. We could only imagine what the neighbors thought. Daniel would throw himself on the floor and wail for a long time. It was difficult to soothe him. We tried the idea of walking away and letting him scream it out, but that seemed to make it worse. Perhaps he needed to be held, even though he didn't want to be. We noticed other unusual behavior. We'd put them in a room for a timeout, one minute per year of their age. They'd scream at the top of their lungs and trash the room and we didn't know why. Later on, we discovered that some of the reasons they were afraid to be in a room alone stemmed from experiences they had, prior to coming into foster care. We tried a modified version of a timeout, having them sit on the floor near our feet. They seemed to be less anxious and angry when timeouts were arranged geographically close to where one of us was sitting. This was our first clue to their obvious social delays, but there were others.

They didn't play nicely with other children. They were always fighting and hitting. We had to watch them closely at parks, parties, and family gatherings. They strayed too far from everyone. We'd check on them and they seemed fine, but it seemed the minute we were out of earshot, we were getting reports that they were being verbally and physically aggressive. Between watching them with food and other children; we were becoming extremely hypervigilant. Once, we were camping, and little four-year-old Chip stood on his tippy toes, nose-to-nose with a much bigger boy ready to take him on. I stepped in between them before he got pounded to the ground, pulling him away from the boy as he shouted back nasty names at him. He never knew when to quit! We worried that he'd meet his match and be on the losing end of a bad brawl, before he learned when to walk away from a disagreement. But if daytime issues were difficult, night time was even worse.

The boys were afraid of the dark. They would not sleep by themselves. I tried rocking them one at a time in the rocking chair. It was something that I very much enjoyed with my biological kids. They didn't want to be held and rocked. It took hours to get Chip to stay in bed, but we eventually managed to get him to sleep in his bed. However, he kept sneaking out of bed and we had to keep shooing him back in. Dan was even more difficult to get to sleep and we couldn't put them in the same room. We would have been up all night long. The only way that we found to comfort Dan, was to put a crib mattress on the floor in our room, made up with pillows and blankets as a makeshift bed. For whatever reason, he didn't want to be held or rocked, but he didn't want to be too far away from us either. By using this little bed, he felt close enough to feel safe and secure. He just wouldn't sleep anywhere else. When you get exhausted enough, you try anything. Years later, we asked him to try to sleep in his bedroom, but left the mattress in our room. We told him he could always come down if he felt he needed to during the middle of the night. For the next year or two, we'd awake every morning to find him asleep and curled up on his little bed. Somewhere along the way, he stopped coming down.

Both boys were sneaky to a degree I'd never witnessed before. No matter what we told them or how many times we'd told them something, they did whatever they wanted anyway. They didn't seem to have the trust that is inherent between a parent and a biological child. They didn't want or need our counsel, even when they were very young. They wanted to rely on their own understanding, always preferring to learn things the hard way. Even when they were proven wrong, they still didn't want to admit it. I'd known kids to lie about things that would get them into trouble, if they told the truth. However, I hadn't known kids to lie for no reason at all; but Chip and Daniel lied without reason. They could lie straight to our faces even when they knew we knew the truth and try to convince us that we were wrong. They were also very deceitful. They went out of their way to defy us. While they could be extremely belligerent and defiant, at the same time, they had no trouble asking us for things they wanted. They asked for things that were outrageously expensive or that they knew they weren't allowed to have.

It soon became apparent just how much they were in need of time and attention. They were sickly, constantly hungry, and completely bouncing off the walls. The daycare was calling often enough that it was beginning to affect my job. At about the peak of my frustration, my husband took a job working as a traveling carpenter. It was time for me to quit my job and devote myself to our children's needs.

Public School Failure

Just prior to the adoption, it was time for Chip to go to school and off he went for two and half hours of Kindergarten at our local public school. He had a great time at school. His teacher did not. He wouldn't sit in his chair, not even for a minute. He couldn't sit still for a picture book story. At snack time, he'd wolf down his portion before he was off and racing around. The other students weren't learning a thing due to his disruption and neither was he. He was constantly in trouble and wouldn't accept a consequence. He was in the office more than he was in the classroom. I was getting phone calls from his teacher or the principal weekly, if not daily. After the phone call in which the principal relayed that he'd been sent to the office and was found doing cartwheels down the halls, disrupting all the other classes along the way; we decided maybe it was time for plan B. Maybe he needed more time to settle into our family. Maybe he needed another year of maturity under his belt. We weren't really sure of the reason for his inability to sit still for more than 30 seconds in that classroom, but we were sure of one thing: it just wasn't working out.

We began to question if he needed to be in school at all. He was a young Kindergartener. By law, we weren't required to even send him to school until he was 7 years old. Since he wasn't learning anything anyway, we made the decision to dis-enroll him from Kindergarten. I also knew that we couldn't plop him right back into Kindergarten or first grade without some educational foundation. We didn't want him to be far behind the other students by the time he re-entered school. I would need to do a pre-school program for him at home. In developing an educational plan for him, I had a lot of work ahead of me.

A fair number of the families at our church were homeschool families. This was a new concept for me. I had to admit that all the homeschool families that I knew, the kids were responsible, personable, and well adjusted. I liked them. I also learned that while it was not an overly popular idea for the time, it was completely legal. Inquisitively, I interviewed a number of the parents who homeschooled their kids. What did they like about it? What problems did they face? What advice did they have to offer? Initially, I was apprehensive at the notion. I was a business woman, who knew nothing about teaching. In sharing my fears with another mother, who'd been homeschooling for years, she asked me a very basic question, "Do you love your kids?"

I uttered a bewildered reply, "Of course!"

She patted my hand and gently responded by saying, "Then you can homeschool your kids, because that's really all it takes." Having that conversation gave me the courage to take the plunge into the world of homeschooling. We certainly had nothing to lose by trying it. After all, Chip and I would both be home all day, anyway. Even if he only learned a little bit each day, it would be better than nothing at all. So, I inquired of the other homeschooling families about which curriculums were the best to use and where they purchased them. After researching several programs, I settled on one I liked.

Homeschool Success

Now it was time to tell Chip about this new addition to our daily schedule. When I told him we were going to do school work for an hour a day, he was pretty excited. It was not doing schoolwork and learning about new things that excited him. It was the one hour every day of my undivided attention that he was elated about. He kept asking me if this time was 'just for him, without the other kids." I assured him it would be. When we actually started I learned a few more things about abused and neglected kids.

The program I selected utilized a lot of singing. I chose it for several reasons. Other families liked it and told me it helped form a solid base for reading. I thought the musical aspect of it would make learning fun.

Chip was very excited the first day of homeschool. He eagerly sat next to me, and was as attentive and astute as any student could be. This was *his* special time and he intended to enjoy every minute of it. Through trial and error, I discovered that he couldn't remember things without a lot of repetition however, he could remember them if we sang them. This was an easy fix. Singing is a mnemonic device which works well for remembering lessons. We began to use songs to tackle more difficult subjects or when he'd get stuck on something. Within five weeks, this little boy who couldn't sit still for 30 seconds was actually reading basic story books. I took him back to the school for speech therapy and the school was stunned! They couldn't imagine that I'd gotten him to sit still long enough to learn anything. In reality, it had nothing to do with *his* ability to *pay* attention. It had everything to do *my* ability to *give* attention. The first step with homeschooling gave me the confidence I needed to take the second step.

Since homeschooling was going so well with Chip, I added a pre-school program for Daniel. By the next fall, Samantha and Mason were anxious to be homeschooled as well. With my husband traveling doing construction, we surmised that this might be a window of opportunity for learning via living history.

If we traveled with Jim some of the time, it would help us stay connected as a family, as well as provide a hands-on learning experience for the kids. In short order, I learned how to develop my own unit studies surrounding whatever city he was working in. We bought a large motorhome equipped with bath and kitchen facilities. When we traveled, we studied in the camper in the morning and then traipsed off to see all the wonders that we'd learned about earlier. We studied the Revolutionary War in Boston and the Civil War in Mobile, Alabama. We danced with Native American Indians in New Mexico and explored the Grand Canyon. During camping trips, I sometimes let the forest rangers do the teaching. They were generally happy to be of service, especially during the off-seasons, when they were less busy. At home, between travels, we packed our books in our backpacks, hopped on our bicycles and completed our schoolwork in the forest preserve. We re-experienced history. The world was our classroom.

We also learned to live minimally. Each of us had our own cubby in the camper with seven day's worth of clothing. Our meals were simply a basic cut of meat with fresh fruits and vegetables from the farmer's markets. We had a television, but we never watched it much. In the evenings, we played board games and card games. We rode bicycles, took walks, and connected with one another around a campfire. It was a simple life, but a good life.

When my husband took a job closer to our home, our traveling days were over. I asked the kids if they were ready to go back to school. It was a resounding and unanimous, "No!" I continued to homeschool all four of my children for a total of eight years. It was physically, emotionally, and intellectually taxing for me at times, but overall, I hold fond memories of that chapter of my life. I don't regret a moment of time that I spent with my children. The woman at church who told me that the only requirement for homeschooling your kids was love, was absolutely right. As much as I enjoyed it, we continued to struggle through some of the problems that the boys were having. There was something unusual going on with Chip.

Manic Rages

Every once in a while, Chip would go into such a meltdown, it was hard to imagine what happened to the happy-go-lucky kid, that we usually saw. It was as if he transformed into an entirely different child, and not a nice one at that. It would start off with a normal defiance to something he objected to, but then it would escalate to something much, much, bigger. He experienced rages where he'd kick me and hit me and bite me. He'd spit at me, blow mucus into my hair, and even threaten to rob a bank and kill me. He'd take off running down the street. It lasted for hours. When the rage was over, he'd curl up in my lap afterwards and shake uncontrollably for another hour. I'd never seen anything like it. It was much more than any temper tantrum I'd ever seen. It was exhausting! We took him to a counselor, who told us it was just normal adoption issues. We had some testing done, which showed nothing. We had more counseling, but it wasn't getting better. Rages didn't happen every day or even every week, but they did seem to occur on a regular basis. I began to record the rages on the calendar and discovered an interesting pattern. They were happening about every 28–34 days, or approximately, once a month. They were always the same and they always lasted about 3 hours. Over time, I could see the mania coming over him like an evolving tornado and braced myself for the worst. I began to wear out emotionally.

I was stressed to my wits end. It was taking a 3 hour chunk of school time away from the other kids once a month. We had a safety plan for the times he raged. My daughter would seclude the other children and the dog in another room so that he could not hurt them, while I dealt with Chip as best I could. When it was over, the other children were emotionally drained and upset. I increasingly felt emotionally beaten down by his verbal and physical abuse towards me. It was the first time I questioned myself if I could really parent him long term. Was I equipped? Was I strong enough to do it? We decided I needed a break. We decided to enroll him in a private Christian school, so that the other kids and I could have a break from the rages.

Also, during this time, Chip played on an ice hockey team. We noticed that when he was manic, he played hockey better than anyone on either team. He could move faster and make moves that no one else his age could do. While it helped his hockey game, the rages were making us miserable. We set up even more counseling and testing.

Daniel was becoming more and more defiant. He was still fighting with peers. His issues were daily, not monthly, and they were getting worse. We decided to take both boys for extensive psychological testing.

I told the clinician who tested Chip that there was something wrong with him. We didn't know what it was, but it was something more than adoptive issues. This time, they asked me, if I had to guess, what did I think it was? It seemed such an odd question to me. They were the experts. I didn't want to suggest that it was something and have them prove me right. I wanted *them* to tell *me* what it was. I had been researching his symptoms and it all looked a lot like my mother and sister's bipolar disorder. "If I had to guess, I'd say it looks like mania," I told them. They told me that they'd never, ever diagnose such a small child with bipolar disorder. It's best not to "label" them too early and have them be stuck with such a diagnosis for a lifetime. When the results came in, they would not disclose them to me over the phone. They would only tell me in person. When I went in for the consultation, the therapist looked at me soberly, "Your son has bipolar disorder." I repeated her earlier comment about never, ever making this diagnosis at his age. She told me that they don't and that in this case, it was clear. He had it. I needed to find a psychiatrist. He needed medication.

Recovery

In 2004, we took him to a psychiatrist who took his history and then ordered an EEG (electroencephalogram), which records changes in brainwave activity. The doctor asked us to schedule it right around the time that Chip was likely to have a manic episode, and we'd need to keep him awake all night long, the night prior to testing. We took shifts sleeping and entertaining him the night before the test. The results were abnormal. The psychiatrist prescribed a mild mood stabilizer. He did have another manic episode, but it was milder with less duration. His doctor increased the dosage. The next episode was even milder. He increased it some more. We passed the 30 day mark, no meltdown. 45 days, still holding my breath. 60 days, did we get it? 75 days, no more rages. He has been stable for many years now and continues to live a happy and productive life. After 6 years and 72 rages, Chip's bipolar disorder was stabilized. Recovery from mental illness leaves a devastating scar on the person who has it, but it also leaves deep scars on the people who love them.

Healing and Rebuilding

In our family, the person most deeply scarred, was me. The rages almost always occurred when my husband was at work, leaving me to deal with them. I was the one who had been verbally and physically attacked for six years. I had some emotional wounds to recover from. It took time for me to recognize the stable Chip. I had to re-teach myself how to speak to him and how to respond to him. At first, I was reluctant to take the walls down, anticipating that he was going to attack me. I had to consciously think about communicating with him in a new way, a better way. It was difficult to break my own bad habits, but over time, we developed a close and loving mother-son relationship. He was worth everything we went through. Through the hard work of attaining stabilization and recovery, he has a bright and wonderful future. I love him so much and appreciate all the wonderful things about him. He is one of the many blessings of my life.

Chapter Four

DIAGNOSING TRAUMA AND MENTAL ILLNESS IN DANIEL

FROM OUR TRAINING, WE remembered that kids could have different developmental ages. The boys proved to be a valid case study. In comparison to their chronological ages, their physical ages were right on target. Intellectually, they were a bit delayed, but coming along. Socially and emotionally, they were several years younger. We wondered if it would ever level out. Daniel was also having severe problems.

It didn't really look like mania. We didn't know what it was. Neither did the therapists. The same set of testing that so clearly diagnosed Chip's bipolar disorder, yielded nothing for Daniel. His chart listed his diagnosis as Oppositional-Defiant disorder and they recommended counseling. In spite of added counseling sessions, his behavior escalated.

The screaming never lessened, even as he got older. It continued through the first part of middle school and then it gradually gave way to verbal abuse. When he didn't get his way or like what someone said, he'd unload on them verbally. When someone didn't respond the way he wanted them to or give in to his unrealistic demands; he'd blindside them with a barrage of curse words. If he construed that someone put him down, even if they hadn't, but he had the perception that he'd been put down, he'd seek revenge by belittling them and demeaning them. He played dirty. There was no limit to how low he'd stoop to hurt someone emotionally. He'd generally sense the person's weakest personality trait, biggest fear, or deepest hurt and use it against them. I recall an incident when he was very small, maybe about three or four years old. I don't remember exactly what he did; just that it reeked of getting even. It's unusual for such a small child to have such thoughts and it really took me by surprise. It was what he said under his breath after I confronted him about it that took my breath away. He smirked, "Ha, ha, double surprise." It was chilling.

He was also physically abusive. Out of the blue, he'd grab whatever was closest to him and whip it at a person. Sometimes he aimed at walls or windows. He was breaking and damaging a lot of things in the house. He was sneaky, deceitful, and vengeful. Other children would come over to play, but within 15 minutes of playing together, it always ended with Daniel shouting at them, calling them names, and throwing things at them. Children were scrambling away from our yard on a regular basis.

He bullied them. Other children avoided coming to our house out of fear. He had to be supervised closely during home school group events. One of our neighbors was his teacher at the pre-school. As we chatted outside one day, she shared with me something unusual that he did at school. He would gather the kids together and give them instructions. The instructions didn't make any rational sense. It wasn't any kind of organized or recognizable game. At the time, neither our neighbor nor I could figure out exactly what it was he was doing. Years later, I came to realize that he was grooming them so that he could bully them. He wanted to be in control over his peers.

When he was about five years old, he wanted to play ice hockey like his brothers, so we put him on a team. After the first game, the teams lined up facing each other to shake hockey gloves. I saw Daniel turn to face the boy behind him. I panicked. I knew what was coming. I flew out of the stands, opened the ice rink door, flew across the ice, slipping and sliding to catch Daniel's fist on the back swing, before his fist struck the other boy's helmet. I picked up my son and carried him off the ice, with him kicking and screaming, and his stick, helmet, and gloves flying. I sat him down on the bench. He was screaming and swearing at me, "You can't do that to me, you're not my coach!"

I said, "I'm your mother and I just did!"

Years later, as we watched the movie, "The Blind Side," we reminisced about that hockey incident. "The Blind Side" details the life of football star, Michael Oher, and his life with Leigh Anne Touhy, the woman who'd taken him off the streets and into her home. When they couldn't get him to understand the game, she marched onto the football field, right past the football coach, and set her new son, Michael Oher straight, as his astonished coach watched her from a distance. When the movie was released, Chip and Daniel treated me to see it. Nearly every scene with Leigh Anne Touhy reminded them of me. Just like in the movie, even though Michael Oher had been received into a loving family home, he still had a bond with his old gang and drug-ridden neighborhood. He had a trauma bond.

Trauma Bond

Chip and Daniel's behavior was much worse when they played with each other, though Chip often did better with his peers than Daniel. The same scenario played out each and every time. They'd be playing with little cars or some other little objects. Daniel would get a sheepish grin on his face. This was the trigger to start crashing the toys and blowing things up. Then they'd start pushing and shoving and fighting with each other. It happened every time they played together. It was far worse when an adult was not in close proximity. It wasn't until their teens that we learned the name for this behavior. It was called a trauma bond. They had lived together in chaos, so when they played together, if it didn't exist on its own, they tried to create it. They took combined comfort in chaos and unrest. In a lesser form, it is not unlike a hostage who sympathizes with his captor or a rape victim who sympathizes with her rapist. An unhealthy emotional tie develops between the victimizer and the victim. Trauma bonds are characterized by an imbalance of power as well as denial of abuse by the victim. The trauma connects them. Nevertheless, the caseworkers told us that they'd settle in, over time, and we really believed that they would.

Homeschool

The patterns of verbal and physical abuse towards Daniel's peers continued in homeschool groups and other enrichment activities. He behaved badly in large groups of children. While his social skills didn't seem to be improving, his intellectual and creative juices were really flowing. Overall, he enjoyed homeschool and like his brother; he enjoyed spending time with me.

I'll share a homeschooling secret. Homeschoolers don't stay home. I'm sure there are some who sit at the kitchen table, but the vast majority that I know embrace the same philosophy that we had: "The World is Your Classroom." Our classroom became anywhere that we could learn about something. Thus, we belonged to a homeschool group that did a wide variety of activities including classes in art, speech, gym, drama, science, Spanish, and others. Daniel was a troublemaker amongst his peers, often disrupting his classes. The larger the group, the larger the problems I had with him. It was difficult to enjoy friendships with other mothers because I had to stand vigil with Daniel. I was afraid to take my eyes off of him for fear that he'd hurt someone. Parents are in abundance during homeschool groups, giving me the benefit of strong supervision. This made it difficult for him to get away with as much as he might have otherwise. While he continued to struggle socially, he was blossoming creatively.

For the most part, Daniel enjoyed homeschool. He was highly intelligent, which works to the youngest child's advantage in a homeschool class. The older kids were 2–5 grade levels above him. While I was teaching the older kids their lessons, he was learning right along with them, soaking it all up like a sponge. When we were doing learning activities outside of our home, I had to teach to my daughter's level, which was the highest level. Over the eight years that we spent in this educational setting, Daniel's educational base became quite strong. A common trait amongst children who were abused or neglected during infancy or early childhood is that they have brain damage to the frontal lobe, which channels emotions and cause-and-effect reasoning. The part of the brain that affects emotions develops during infancy. When it is not stimulated through parental love and attention, it fails to develop. Kids like Daniel can be highly intelligent, yet have a severe inability to regulate every day emotions. Clinicians have long commented how he can explain his disorders to them as if he'd taken college psychology courses, yet he was unable to respond as he knew society expected him to.

The other secret about homeschooling is that there is little wasted time. Students don't waste learning time lining up for a drink of water, taking a bathroom break or changing classrooms. Most homeschool curriculum can be completed in about 2 ½ hours, leaving a large amount of time for other activities.

Focusing on Strengths

Having large amounts of time to devote to creative pursuits was one of Daniel's biggest assets with regard to homeschool. He filled up much of his days mastering drawing, playing piano, and dancing.

From the time Daniel was two years old, he could feel and hear music in his head. I vividly recall standing at the sink washing dishes with Daniel sitting at my feet, playing with cars. I like to have the radio on when I'm doing household chores and that day was no exception. I began singing along to "The Lion Sleeps Tonight." "In the village, the mighty village, the lion sleeps tonight…" As I was standing there, I glanced down at Daniel, who was playing with small cars near my feet. I heard this little voice harmonizing with me. "A weemowhip, a weemowhip." Was this two year old singing along with me? I continued singing to see if he'd keep going. He never even looked up at me. He just kept nonchalantly playing with his cars and singing along. I was amazed! This was some talent. As he got older, we experimented with him in various sports, but nothing really clicked for him. He was a decent athlete but it was clear he'd never rival his older brothers in the sports arena. However, his talents in the creative arts were jaw dropping.

He did seem to enjoy many of the same things his sister enjoyed, notably piano and Irish Dance. At the age of eight, he started piano lessons. Within months, he was playing pieces his sister had taken years to master. She got frustrated and quit. He blossomed. He was composing pieces within the first year, even writing them on paper and submitting them to composition contests. We'd sit with the other parents at the piano recitals politely clapping for each player whether it was a good or bad performance. When Daniel would play, we could hear people gasping and saying, "He's really good! What an amazing talent!" His piano teacher adored him. She had told me that she had to coax her students to open the music and get started. She would get such a kick out of Daniel, who would come into her house, sit at the piano, whip open the music and start playing like mad. It gave her immense joy to watch him. At the same time, she was often frustrated with him because she'd tried to teach him to play according to how the music was written and he was always jazzing things up. Musing to herself, she secretly enjoyed his versions of the music. Some of his favorite pieces were Irish folk songs.

Daniel was also an Irish Dancer. This was yet another area in which he quickly surpassed his sister's efforts. His dance teacher once told the entire class that Daniel had all the makings of a world class Irish Dancer. Since there are very few boys in Irish Dance, she was thrilled to have him. There was just one problem for Daniel. There were thousands of people at the Irish Dance competitions and this was just the type of situation to cause him to be aggressive. He'd get disoriented. He kept disappearing. I'd tell him one thing, he'd do another. He was hypervigilant. His speech didn't make sense. He'd line up for the girls-only dances and forget who his partner was. Yet, having such natural creative talent combined with having natural rhythm, yielded other benefits.

Our daughter, Samantha, was doing a lot of scholarship pageants at the time. Often, they would include talent contests. She'd bounce ideas for choreography off Daniel, who seemed to have a knack for knowing what was eye-catching on stage. He began to coach her in the areas of modeling and talent. She'd usually win. Other contestants would inquire as to who her coach was. They'd be surprised to learn it was just her little brother.

Daniel is also an amazing artist. He could draw almost anything. Our good friend, Topper Helmers, freelance commercial artist and illustrator of this book cover, visited us and took the time to have a mini art lesson with Daniel. He sat and drew with Daniel and taught him some tricks of the trade, while sharing all the in's and out's of preparing for a career as a commercial artist. Topper commented that Daniel had more artistic talent than he had at the same age. He also pointed out that freelance artwork was a viable option for a boy with his issues. Artists work when the creative spirit moves them or when they have deadlines to meet. He suggested Daniel should consider this type of work because he could work when he felt in good spirits and take time off when he was not. We all took note of his valuable advice.

Public school

In 2005, the economy started to decline. I had to return to work. Our homeschooling days were over. We put all four kids into public school for the first time. The older three adapted pretty well. Emotionally, Daniel fell completely apart.

He was regularly in trouble in class and on the bus. By the time he got to his locker, he was so stressed out; he couldn't even think clearly enough to grab books and materials for class. Within six weeks of entering the fifth grade, we had to admit Daniel to the psychiatric ward for the first time, for danger to self and others.

A fair amount of the time he could hold it together at school. However, his formerly good grades, began to nosedive. At home, he became violent and aggressive. He damaged property on his way home from the bus. He tried to fight other kids. He ripped the mailbox off the post and slammed it through a window. He had begun cussing intolerably, constantly screaming, and swearing. He turned the steering wheel when we were driving, trying to force us into oncoming traffic, to get even for not getting his way. He whipped objects at us, as we drove the car.

School was stressing him out. What was it about school that triggered past abuse and neglect? It was something sensory. Sights, sounds, smells, visions, what? Something was triggering him to feel severe anxiety. We began counseling and family therapy. In 6th grade, the students had to change classes for all the subjects. His behavior escalated further. He was stressed with so many kids at the bus stop. Then, he was on a noisy, crowded bus. After that, he waited outside the school building for about 15 minutes with 500 students before the school opened up. By the time he got to his locker, he was so emotionally disregulated, he couldn't put materials into the locker or get things out for his first class. He jammed the locker shut, trapping things in the door. His locker was so bent and beaten up; he had to have a teacher help him with it every day. When he became too embarrassed to get help, he went to class with nothing and took a zero. His grades were faltering and were noticeably worse towards the end of the day. Meanwhile, his creative energies took a turn towards the dark side.

Daniel wrote songs and stories. In the past, he liked a wide variety of music, from Elvis to contemporary Christian, and from folk songs and ballads to rock and roll. Now he liked rap. He enjoyed writing his own rap songs, which were filled with racial slurs and curse words. He wrote about killing people and the power of money. He drew violent images in cartoon with weird faces and fierce weapons. He made threats in writing. He seemed fixated on evil things.

Along with the fixation on evil and corrupt ideations came increased verbal and physical abuse. He was defiant, daily. He cursed constantly despite any kind of consequence. He was angry at anything and everything. He was angry there was no cereal for breakfast even though there were plenty of other choices. He was deceitful and manipulative. He lied about everything. We didn't trust him walking down the hall. He targeted Chip, as he usually targeted whoever was physically smaller or emotionally weaker. He'd whisper insults at him under his breath just out of our earshot.

We hired an after school caregiver, who was a Certified Nursing Assistant, to supervise him for a couple of hours after school. Daniel saw this as an opportunity to get away with a lot of things. We often called the police for help. The other children were never sure when he'd lash out at them or someone else and they'd have to run to safety.

I called the school to request a meeting. We needed to get an Individualized Education Plan (IEP) in place for him. My good friend, Randie, who is an attorney, offered to attend the meeting with me. The IEP meeting was in the morning. By profession, I am an insurance agent and generally wear business suits to work. Randie was on her way to court, so we both arrived in sharp looking business suits. We inquired about the meeting at the desk. They showed us to the small conference room and explained that they were ready. They were just waiting for the parents to arrive. I said, "I am Daniel's mother." Obviously flustered, the receptionist stammered a response, "You just look so, so, professional!" Randie whispered to me, "I think they expected you to have on jeans and t-shirt and look like you just rolled out of bed." Ultimately that meeting resulted in an IEP, as well as a placement in a therapeutic day school for Daniel, but things didn't get better there either.

Daniel's therapist suggested that we have a neuro-psychological test done. The results were fairly normal, except for some notations about mild, executive function weakness. We took him to a psychiatrist, started him on medications, and continued therapy.

It was about this juncture that we came to several conclusions. Some kids, like Chip, could be stabilized with medication and therapy. Both boys had more success with homeschool in comparison with public school. Daniel could not manage public school at all.

In reviewing our initial thoughts regarding adopting kids with mental illness, now that we had them, we were thankful that my mother and sister had taught us a few things about mental illness. They had made it far easier for us to recognize the symptoms of mental illness in our sons. As a foster-adopt parent, having extended family members with mental illness was far more an asset, than a liability. The final lesson in all this, and perhaps the scariest lesson, is that we began to feel as though we were in over our heads.

We had closed the door to our safe and secure little homeschool. We had opened the door to public school, and we were soon to be stuck in the psychiatric revolving door.

"In my mind, there's nothing our generation should be more ashamed of than people with severe mental illness being punished for a disease they can't do anything about."

Fran Quigley

Chapter Five

THE PSYCHIATRIC REVOLVING DOOR

WE PUT THE LOCAL CRISIS team phone number on speed dial. Often, we had to call 911 first. We developed our own family safety plan. When Daniel was violent, there was a three step process.

1. Duck
2. Run to safety
3. Call 911

We trained our other children to respond to one of his outbursts in the same way most families practice for a fire drill. Subsequently, the same chain of events followed the "safety plan," calls to the crisis team, and 911.

We tried to de-escalate Daniel and keep ourselves safe, until the crisis worker arrived. We'd answer questions for an hour or longer. The on-call worker would decide if hospitalization was warranted. It usually was. We spent several more hours trying to get the admission approved, the paperwork completed, and finding a hospital with an open bed. Then there was always the decision of how to transport him safely. Could we safely drive him there? Did we need an ambulance? We waited several more hours while the crisis worker set up transportation and an ambulance arrived. Then there was another hour-long drive to the facility and a few more hours spent getting him admitted. Upon exiting the hospital revolving door, we noticed the sun was coming up. We'd been at this all night long. He was admitted and discharged through that revolving door 11 times within 2 years. We were exhausted.

My husband and I decided to take turns doing the hospital runs, so that only one of us had to go to work after a sleepless night. While we were trying to keep ourselves awake during working hours, the hospital staff took pity on the patient who'd been up all night and allowed him to sleep all day. Before we'd have a chance to go home and grab even a small nap, the hospital expected us to drive another hour to participate in a "family session" as required by the insurance company. I'm certain the therapists were all trained at the same college. They all asked the same questions in the family session. What do your parents do that make it worse for you? What do they do that makes it better for you? What do you need to do, Daniel? Are you ready to do it differently? Six different hospitals, a dozen different therapists. They all asked the same questions.

Life was far easier on Daniel. If the next day or two was a weekend, most of the treatment staff was not even there. He usually did get a bit of therapy, and if we were lucky, they might have had time to connect with his regular psychiatrist to adjust meds. Daniel's anxiety had quelled by the time he was admitted, so he enjoyed his stay in the psychiatric ward watching television, playing video games, and enjoying the food. Meanwhile, mom or dad was driving home with the radio blaring in order to stay awake long enough to drive home. Four days later, he was discharged.

Two of the hospitals were very honest with us. We don't know how to help him. Don't bring him back here. We looked at the map. How many behavioral health hospitals were in the Chicagoland area? What would we do when they all refused him?

Speaking of honesty, a therapist at one of those hospitals dared to say what no one else would. It happened on one of those "toothpicks to hold open the eyelid" trips to do a family session. Hospital therapists sometimes had mercy on us and allowed us to do the family session via teleconference. This particular therapist insisted I do the family session in person. That would mean an hour drive there and an hour drive back home. I was already exhausted. I'd been up all night. I worked all day. I had other kids at home I needed to see. I pleaded with her to let me do the family session on the phone. We'd done it that way before. No, she insisted that I had to be there in person. I was frustrated, annoyed, short-tempered, and completely depleted. I pushed the revolving door open and was ushered into a small therapy room furnished with a few chairs. The therapist brought Daniel in for the usual family session questions. This therapist had the questions down pat. It was textbook. While we were talking, we could hear yelling and pounding on the wall from an adjacent room. We heard screaming, swearing, and sounds of a physical struggle. The therapist tried to ignore it and continue with the session, but she was noticeably uncomfortable. I sat stone faced. Daniel tried to refrain from smiling. After a blow hit the wall, causing the room to shake, she apologized for the outburst. I replied, "Who would I be to judge someone else's child? My son acts like that!" I was fairly unresponsive to her questions that day. I was just too spent to deal with it. If she was focused; she would have recognized that. She criticized me, "What *is* your problem?"

I glared at her, "My problem is that I'm exhausted and I'm frustrated because we keep bringing him to these places thinking we're going to get some help and all we get is another trip back here in 30 days. She asked me if I really wanted help for my son. Gritting my teeth, I said, "YES! That is why I brought him here!"

She stated flatly, "Then move to Canada, because you are not going to get it here." I was dumbfounded.

I relayed that discussion to our regular therapists. They all told me to report her. I thought about it. I could think of a lot of reasons to report her. Ultimately, there was one very good reason I didn't do it. How I could fault her, when she was the only one who had the moxie to simply tell me the truth?

Each hospital tried to set his discharge up for success at home. Usually, we added another therapy to the litany of those we already had: psychiatry, individual therapy, family therapy, EMDR therapy, therapeutic school, art therapy, music therapy, play therapy, tai chi, and respite. Essentially, we had therapy in one form or another every single day. Still, we were calling 911 and spinning in the psychiatric revolving door.

Every therapist began to ask us the same question. "Have you considered a residential placement?" In fact, we had. We learned that the cost of such treatment was exorbitant, currently costing between $150,000–$180,000 per year. We called our insurance company. Not covered. We called Medicaid. Not covered. We applied for an individualized care grant. Not qualified. We sought advice from our adoption subsidy worker. She had none to offer. We consulted with the Department of Children and Family Services educational liaison. He didn't have any advice either, but he did assist us with one important thing; Daniel's diagnosis.

With every hospitalization, they kept adding additional diagnoses, until we ended up with the whole alphabet soup: ADHD, OCD, ODD, SED, BD, CD, bipolar, and severe anxiety. After carefully listening to our concerns, he enlightened us to a crucial diagnosis. He asked us this, "If your son seemingly has all the symptoms of all the disorders all at the same time, why is it that he doesn't have any of them at all when he's not anxious? It's because what he really has is PTSD, or post-traumatic stress disorder." It was the first thing anyone ever said that actually made sense.

We took that diagnosis to his therapists and they all agreed that Daniel had PTSD. So, we finally had an accurate diagnosis. We had an appropriate treatment recommendation. He needed residential treatment. But how did we move away from the psychiatric revolving door towards the main entrance of residential treatment? There was no access to this treatment and certainly no funding to pay for it.

Notes from my journal as Daniel's behavior escalated to a dangerous level.

December 14, 2007–There was snow. Daniel wanted to snowboard. I told him okay, but let's try it for about an hour. Try to have a success. I'll call you in one hour. If it all goes well, have some lunch and you may go out again later. There were a lot of kids out there playing. I was worried he might hurt someone. I couldn't relax. I kept looking out the window for signs of fighting. The hour was up. I called him three times, but he ignored me. I would have to go get him. He charged at me and kicked snow in my face, yelling: "Fuck you! Fuck you! You fucking bitch!" He ripped the Christmas wreath off the front door and slammed it down on his way in.

December 15, 2007—The therapeutic school decided he needed to ride in a cab alone coming back from school. The afternoon driver on the mini school bus could not handle his behavior.

January 14–18, 2008—He was sliding again. He wouldn't get up for school in the morning. He was blatantly doing things we have asked him not to do, then swearing at us, being disrespectful, hateful, and mean to everyone in the family.

January 27, 2008—He was obsessing over buying an electronic game. He was having a lot of tantrums. He was whining and crying constantly. He has done over $600 worth of damage to our home.

February 9, 2008—He was suspended from school for pretending to pull a gun on the morning bus driver. We received his progress report. His grades dropped from A's and B's to D's and F's. And some people thought homeschooling was a bad idea.

February 11, 2008—His teacher called. He has been doing his classmate's homework. He was academically ahead of them. He was using this as leverage so he could bully them and get them to do what he wants. He is trying to elevate himself above the biggest troublemaker of the class.

February 14, 2008—Valentine's Day—He often acted up on holidays. I was at work. I got a frantic call from my daughter. Dan had grabbed a large knife from the kitchen. He held it to Chip's throat and threatened to "shank him." She and our other son, Mason, had jumped on him and tried to pull the knife from his hand. It hit the wall with such force; it frightened the afterschool caregiver we'd hired. The caregiver would not call 911. I told my managers I had an emergency at home and raced out of the door. I made three phone calls on my way, as I walked out of the office. First, 911; second, the CARES hotline to report a crisis. I reminded myself to put the CARES number on my cell phone speed dial. Third, I called Randie. I was frantic. What do I do now? Should I let the police arrest him? He was only 13 years old. Randie reminded me that the juvenile justice system was imperfect. Since Daniel had made homicidal and suicidal comments before, she did not want him in juvenile detention. They'd be harsh on him, treating him like a criminal. He wasn't one. The criminal behavior was a direct result of an emotional disorder. How would I feel if his anxiety reached a level where he killed someone or himself? SASS, the crisis team, admitted him to the hospital once again. It was the 10th time in two years. And once again, it happened on a holiday. The prior time was Thanksgiving and the time before that, Halloween.

February 18, 2008—He was released from the hospital. We were all beyond stressed. Jim and I had a tearful conversation about how to keep everyone safe. We decided he could not work. He had to be home to keep everyone safe. Jim's parents have a condo in the next county that they don't use in the winter. He called them to ask if we could use it to split our household and protect the other kids. They gave permission. We planned for me and the other kids to move in there. They didn't want to go. Jim would live with Daniel at our house through the week and I would live with the other kids in the condo. On the weekend, Jim and I would switch places. It felt like divorce.

February 22, 2008—DCFS Trauma Conference—I cleared my calendar to attend it. Representatives from state and local agencies were there. I spoke to someone at the table from SASS, the organization in our state who arranges crisis services at the county level. When she learned how serious our situation was, she connected me with a woman from the Advocacy Department. This woman assessed our situation and suggested that I have our therapist arrange for a clinical staffing with DCFS. I provided the information she'd given me to our therapist on the phone, from my hotel room. Our therapist requested the appointment, but weeks later, we were still not getting a response with a staffing date. He called several more times. Then, he told me to call them. The supervisor screamed at me on the phone and told me that the wrong caseworker had been assigned three times, but he finally fixed it. The staffing was finally held two months later. While we waited for our scheduled appointment, Daniel took two more trips through the psychiatric revolving door.

March 1, 2008–Jim asked Daniel to come in for dinner. He whipped a basketball at Jim's head out of anger. Finally he came in and sat down. He asked Jim to take him to the store to buy an electronic game. Jim said not tonight. Daniel swore at him and dumped an entire pitcher of apple juice on the floor.

March 2, 2008–Some neighbor kids came over to play football. Fifteen minutes later, Daniel was throwing things at them and swearing. They fled. He came in and was swearing at everyone. He kept slamming the front door repeatedly. The frame around the window in the front door broke.

March 6, 2008–While he was at school, he set up a fight with a gang member at a park. He asked the caregiver to leave the park and buy them some snacks. Foolishly, she went. He told Chip to go to a house near the park to meet the gang members for the fight. The gang member had the rest of the gang waiting for them. Chip had no idea what was going on. Someone called the police. The caregiver returned to find them both at risk of being arrested for gang activity. We fired her.

March 14, 2008–The school called and said Daniel was wearing his pants around his rump on purpose. He was being defiant and verbally abusive at school. His teacher acknowledged that they have seen the "mean side" of him. Daniel was physically and verbally abusive towards Jim after school. We contacted our senator to get assistance from the state departments, towards getting Daniel into a residential program. Our senator called Illinois Medicaid to see if they'd cover it. The state department that manages Medicaid denied coverage for residential treatment.

March 15, 2008–His EMDR (eye movement desensitization and reprocessing) therapist escorted me to the bathroom in her office where she showed me marker drawings on the wall. They were explicit and racist. She asked if I thought Daniel had drawn them. Yes, I was sure he had. They were the same phrases he'd been using on a regular basis. She confronted him about it. He asked: "How did you know it was me?" Then he admitted that he'd done it during the last two appointments and that it gave him a "rush." He committed to trying harder, but later that night refused to pick up his cars when asked to do so. He grabbed the plastic container for the cars and shoved it at Jim's face, bloodying his mouth.

March 16, 2008–Another screaming, swearing tantrum occurred. He was angry because Chip looked at him.

March 17, 2008–It is a holiday again, St. Patrick's Day. This was an important holiday for us. We are all Irish. Daniel and Samantha are Irish dancers. After school, Chip came into the house to tell Jim about something inappropriate Daniel had been doing outside. Daniel stormed into the house, picked Chip up, threw him down the stairs, and began beating on him with his fists. Jim had to pull Daniel off of Chip. When I arrived home from work, the police were there and the crisis team was on their way. I asked the SASS worker to follow me outside to my car. I showed her the suitcases in my car. There was one for me and one for each of our other three kids. "This is what it's come to," I told her, "we were ready to split our family, leave, and live in two separate homes to keep the other kids safe. Before I could get them to safety, he'd beaten our other son and we called 911. We can't continue on like this anymore." They admitted him to the psychiatric hospital for the 11th time within 2 years.

March 24, 2008–The hospital wants him discharged. We tried to arrange for a residential placement, but couldn't get funding. The hospital was pressuring us to pick him up.

Chapter Six

THE RELINQUISHMENT: THE DEVIL'S DEAL

IF YOUR CHILD'S LIFE AND future depended upon a treatment that the government denied, and you could not afford to pay for it on your own, forcing you to choose between treatment and custody rights, what choice would you make?

DCFS told us that if we picked him up, they intended to charge us with child endangerment for failure to protect our other children. If we refused to pick him up, they intended to charge us with neglect. They wouldn't give us any other options nor tell us how to resolve our dilemma.

I'm not certain exactly when the first custody relinquishment for mental healthcare happened. I do know that groups of parents came forth from 2003–2005 with the same issue. Why weren't they successful in resolving this issue? Why does it continue a decade later?

The first attempt at resolving custody relinquishment was tackled at the federal level. In 2003, congressmen proposed the Keeping Families Together Act. This Act proposal allotted federal dollars to states, for intensive mental healthcare to eliminate custody relinquishment for mental healthcare.

Its downfall was that it required the states to match federal funds. Many states expressed concern that their budgets could not support it. The bill was defeated. It was reintroduced in 2005. It failed again. The outrage over custody relinquishment quietly dissipated.

In 2008, we found ourselves in the same position as the groups of parents who fought and failed before us. Now we had to choose between doing an illegal thing and an irresponsible thing.

We weighed all the possible choices as carefully as we could. Using foresight, we tried to predict what lay at the end of each path. Which path would give Daniel the treatment he so badly needed while keeping everyone safe? Which path would leave the least negative scar on everyone? Let's walk through the options.

1. **Pay $150,000 per year for treatment.** Could we do this? Could we have a big fundraiser? Could we put a third mortgage on our house? Could we draw from our retirement funds? How many years would we be paying that amount? Even if we pooled all of our funds, we didn't have enough. It was more than our annual combined salaries. We asked the therapists if one year of residential care would be enough. They all said no, without hesitation. A fundraiser would be a lot of work and we were already emotionally spent. Even that would not be enough. Option number one would not work at all.

2. **Have our son arrested and put into juvenile detention.** The court might force him into residential treatment as part of his release. Randie counseled us on the harsh reality of making this choice. He'd be thrown in with juvenile delinquents, gang members, substance abusers, and sex offenders. He'd be treated harshly. Could he survive in this environment? Perhaps, if he were emotionally stable, but he wasn't. In fact, he was extremely unstable. He'd made suicidal and homicidal comments in the past. She asked us to think carefully about making this choice. If he killed himself in there, could we accept that? No, we couldn't. Could we accept him killing someone else? No, we couldn't. Randie was right. Option two would not work either.

3. **Pick him up and bring him home.** How would we keep everyone safe? As it was, Jim had to quit his job because no one else could manage him. We'd have to continue living on my income. Even with one of us home, the other kids were still getting hurt. We could live in two separate dwellings. This would be difficult to do on one income. Our marriage would suffer. The other kids didn't want to live elsewhere. How long would we need to do this? Daniel would not get the residential treatment he needed if we selected this option. We'd still be trapped in the psychiatric revolving door. We couldn't imagine this working out, even for a short period of time.

4. **Refuse to pick him up on the grounds that we couldn't protect our family.** Were they really suggesting that we abandon him at a psychiatric hospital? Did people really do that? Could we do it and live with ourselves knowing we'd done it? We were told that we'd be "scrutinized." We'd be charged with neglect. Perhaps the court would tread lightly on us under the circumstances. Perhaps they'd hit us with both barrels. There were no guarantees. Daniel would be sent to residential care. Our other children would be safe. From a legal perspective, Jim and I would take the fall. We were both emotionally stable. We were likely to endure the legal and emotional fallout better than Daniel.

Those were the only options we could think of at the time. No one offered us any other course of action.

Which one did we choose? Which would you have chosen, give those options? Close your eyes and throw a dart at the map? We thought about it. Pull one of them out of a hat? From all the horrible options to choose from, we chose the only one that would give him the treatment he direly needed and keep everyone safe. The only people who were going to go down, were us. Randie committed to having our backs every step of the way. She couldn't promise that things would go our way. She couldn't protect us from everything. She did promise never to leave our sides. She was the one person who never let us down.

On Thursday, April 1, 2008, Daniel was discharged from the in-patient psychiatric hospital. We told the hospital that we were scheduled to have a meeting with the Illinois Department of Children and Family Services, to see if they could help us gain admission to a residential treatment facility. Would they delay discharge for 2 days, until we met with them? No, they would not. They told us we had to pick him up. They also told us if we didn't come, they'd have to report us to the child abuse hotline for abandonment. After speaking with the therapist, my husband called to tell me that it was best to tell Daniel in person, that we were unable to bring him home for safety reasons. I was at work and too far away to get there in time. My husband entered a small therapy room at the hospital, with a therapist, and our son, Daniel.

Through his tears, he said, "Son, Mom and I love you so much! What we are going to do will hurt you and us very much, but it is something we must do to get you the help you need. We just haven't been able to find any other way to get the money to admit you to a residential treatment facility. It is unsafe for the rest of us to bring you home. This is your only chance. We will not be picking you up. We will be in touch with you as soon as they will let us. A lot of people are going to be coming to talk to you. They will ask you a lot of questions. It is very important that you tell them the truth. At all costs, tell them the truth. We will do our best to know where you are and promise to come see you just as soon as we can. Until then, we want you to know that we love you very, very much and that will never change." Our son cried, the therapist cried. My husband cried all the way home. I cried all the way home too, and I wasn't even there when it all went down. I felt guilty for not being there.

It was time for the revolving door to stop.

We spent the rest of that night in a blur of emotion, which included deep sadness, fear, helplessness, uncertainty, isolation, despair, grief, and so much more. We didn't exactly know what would happen next. It felt like the calm before the storm.

The next day felt so surreal. We knew that the hospital was going to call the DCFS child abuse hotline. We knew we'd be investigated. We knew we'd have to appear in court to explain why we made that choice. We were fearful that we'd just made the biggest mistake of our lives, yet we were hopeful that the court would understand that we weren't given any other option. We had to make the court see, in the very short time allowed, that we had taken such a drastic step to keep everyone safe.

How must a judge rule on a case in which no existing law applies?

On April 2, 2008, a DCFS investigator arrived at our home. Once again, I was at work. The investigator interviewed my husband. He gave her a ream of mental health records several inches thick. He also gave her copies of police reports where we'd made 911 calls to protect ourselves, including the one where Daniel had threatened his brother with a knife. He told her about the scheduled staffing with the DCFS Clinical Department scheduled in two more days and that the hospital had refused our requests to hold him, until a solution could be worked out that would keep everyone safe.

From the investigator's vantage point, she was able to see one hole in the wall. It was the shape of the end of a book. It happened when Dan had whipped a hardcover book at our daughter's head. She ducked. It hit the wall with such force, that the hole in the wall mirrored the size and shape of book end. My husband offered to escort the investigator through our home to view the rest of the damage which pervaded our home, including doors with broken wood frames and doors with door knob locks and dead bolt locks that we installed to prevent Dan from taking the other kids' belongings. He then showed her a hole in the shower enclosure, scratches in the mirror, fibers pulled out of the carpet, a broken wooden stair rail with metal brackets ripped out of the wall, broken windows, smashed window blinds, and gouged woodwork. The exterior door would not line up correctly and the window in the door had a broken frame, causing the window to be loose. Our slider door would never close properly again. The investigator declined to view the rest of the damage. She gave us notice of a juvenile court date and time to appear at a Shelter Care hearing the following day. She never interviewed me at all.

Five minutes later, she called our home and cancelled our Shelter Care court appearance. We didn't know what to make of it. Perhaps they would tell us what to do at the clinical staffing. Perhaps we'd finally get some help. We didn't know if Daniel was still at the hospital or if DCFS picked him up.

If they picked him up, where did they taken him? The investigator refused to tell us. We were completely in the dark.

The next two days, we tried to go about our normal business. We went to work. The other kids went to school. We did laundry. We paid our bills. We bought groceries. But we were mentally preoccupied with thoughts of Daniel. Where *was* he? What must he be thinking? What were they going to do with him? With us? Eventually, we found out that DCFS moved Daniel from the hospital to a temporary crisis center. It seemed like forever before we finally had that clinical staffing—*that fateful day of the clinical staffing.*

On April 3, 2008, we arrived at the DCFS clinical staffing with Randie. Also attending that meeting were two state department representatives, and five therapists. From the state departments were Jean, DCFS clinician, and James, Regional Coordinator of Community and Residential Services Authority (CRSA). CRSA is a state authority designated to offer technical assistance to families of children with severe emotional disorders. They are supposed to be the safety net that "catches" children before they are thrown back into foster care after all the state departments deny funding. Ironically, those who eventually learn about it, also learn that it's "the best kept secret in the state." And even when families learn about it, the CRSA process is simply too slow to be of much useful value to many Illinois families.

Our post adoptive therapist, Ronald, was at a conference, but he teleconferenced in with his supervisor, Judy. Daniel's SASS worker, John, from the county mental health department was there. Daniel's psychologist, Dr. Lisa, was also there. And there was Mindy, the therapist from a local community network center. No one had ever contacted us from this organization before. We were informed that the DCFS investigators were in an adjacent room and that Jean would be meeting with them after the staffing. We were questioned for hours regarding events that occurred starting from the time the boys came to live in our home, all the way up to the 11th hospitalization.

Jean asked all of the therapists if they had any other services to provide us. No, they did not. They had exhausted every service they could think of that may have helped. James, from CRSA, said it was the most extensive wraparound program he'd seen in his career.

Jean informed us that we could not just leave him at a psychiatric hospital. Doing so, was considered abandonment. We reminded her that we'd done so upon the recommendation of a therapist and that we'd done it to protect ourselves from physical harm. She would make a formal recommendation that Daniel be given residential treatment. But there was a catch. No decisions would be made that day. There were other procedures to follow and they all took time. We would not have an answer for three to four months. We'd need to keep ourselves safe in the interim. We shared with the group gathered in that staffing how we'd almost split our family in two to keep everyone safe. If we waited, we'd have to reside in separate dwellings until they came back with an answer. Jean nodded her head profusely. She thought splitting up our family was a good plan and encouraged us to do so. The answer regarding funding might not even be yes. If we were lucky enough to get it, it would only last for 3 months, but we might be able to extend it a couple of times. We could get 11 months maximum. What if he still wasn't stable after the first year? We'd be back at square one. I asked Ronald, if we could keep ourselves safe for four months and could get him into a residential treatment center, would he be stable and safe enough to return home in a year? "No, he said, it will take longer than a year."

Jean asked, "Are you going to continue refusing to pick your son up from the psychiatric hospital?"

I answered, "Can anyone in this room tell us how we can pick him up, get him the treatment he needs, and keep everyone safe at home?"

One by one, they all shook their heads. "No."

"Then, how can we pick him up? We're not equipped. What is the right thing to do? You are asking us to choose between doing an illegal thing and an irresponsible thing."

What transpired next, in that room, was the DCFS version of "hot potato." Jean asked Mindy if her organization could find a place to house him while they initiated processes and protocols to get him into residential treatment. A placement would not be made for months. Where could he go in the interim? Mindy replied that they could not put him in a shelter. He was too violent, too dangerous. The shelters were not locked facilities. The staff was not trained to handle a child with severe disorders. Besides, shelters would only keep him for 48 hours. Then, he'd have to be moved. Jean retorted, "Well, we can't place him in a foster home. Almost all of them have younger children. He could hurt one of them. Mindy suggested a group home. "No," Jean said, "they are not locked facilities either. We'd have the same problem as you have with a shelter." They wanted to know if we could bring him home while they got the placement figured out. I looked at James. His eyes got big and he gave a slight shake of the head as if to say, "Let them figure it out." I turned and glanced at Randie. I knew her glare well enough to know not to say a word. She was sending messages to me via mental telepathy, "Duct tape, duct tape, put some duct tape on your mouth."

I thought to myself, these are the experts. They do this every day. We are just average parents. If they can't figure out where to put him, even for a short while, how in the world were we going to bring him home to three other kids? How differently the landscape looks when they are the ones viewing it. When we had custody and did not have the resources to manage his mental illness, they all looked at us as if we were inept. Yet, when they had responsibility for him, they panicked and bounced him around that room like a rabid ping pong ball. It was all relative based upon who bore the responsibility for managing his behavior.

We left with more questions than we came in with. The investigator called the following day. We had to be in court Tuesday morning for a Shelter Care hearing to answer charges for neglect. Randie said she would not allow us to enter that court room without her. That was *her territory*. Legally, we were in good hands. It was the only good thing we had going for us.

On April 4, 2008, DCFS moved Daniel to a shelter.

Two days later, no one was letting us know if we could see or talk to him. I went to the shelter with some of his clothing. Really, I just wanted to see him and make sure he was all right. He was not there. The staff told me a DCFS worker had taken him somewhere the night before, but they didn't know where. It was only a 48 hour shelter.

We were extremely worried. Where was he? Was he scared? When would they let us see him? What were they trying to accomplish in scaring a boy who was already emotionally compromised? What did they seek to gain by doing this?

Where We Drew the Line

We drew the line where the government should have drawn it for us. Safety. Isn't that the whole purpose of DCFS-safety?

We drew the line at safety.

We chose number 4. The Bazelon Center for Mental Healthcare in Washington D.C. has long called it "barbaric." NAMI, the National Alliance on Mental Illness, has long referred to it by another adjective, "unthinkable." The state governments put a name on it that makes it sound a bit more acceptable to people. They call it, "custody relinquishment for mental healthcare." "Trading custody rights for mental healthcare" has a totally different ring to it, but that is exactly what it is. It is a civil rights violation. We coined our own term for option #4.

"*The Devil's Deal.*"

*"Why should this be treated any
differently than a physical illness?"*
Aaron Rapier, Attorney at Law

Chapter Seven

JUVENILE COURT:
THE CHILD ABUSE LENS

ON APRIL 8, 2008, we appeared at the Shelter Care hearing. We dressed in
business suits per Randie's instruction. We went through the metal detectors
and sat in the court lobby. As I sat there, I had a flashback to a conversation
we'd had with our first adoption worker so long ago. Her words played in my
head. "You need to be sure. This is permanent. We don't want the kids back.
Disrupting or dissolving an adoption is a very painful process for everyone."
How in the world had we arrived at this place?

Ronald, Dan's therapist, came at our request. He wanted the judge to
know that this was not our fault, that we'd done everything we could to
prevent this. He took a seat next to us and Randie. The investigator came
in next. She was dressed in jeans and a sweatshirt. She sat next to us too.
Ronald confronted her about some of the things she'd written in her report
regarding his interview. She'd taken some of what he'd said out of context. He
clarified his meaning for her. She hadn't understood the difference between
"authoritative" and "authoritarian" relative to parenting. The caseworker
stood off in a corner making a call on his cell phone. Our name was called

on the docket and we were ushered into a tiny waiting room adjacent to the court room.

A few minutes later, the door to the court room opened. The bailiff motioned us inside. I took a quick survey of the court room. It felt reminiscently familiar. It hadn't changed since I'd laid my eyes on it nine years prior. This juvenile court building had only two court rooms. The court room we'd entered was the same court room which I had come to more than a decade earlier, when I had advocated for the boys as foster children. I glanced at the chairs at the back and side of the room that I used to sit in back then. Those seats were reserved for the caseworkers, CASA, therapists, foster parents, and any other visitors. Today, my husband and I would not sit at the back with the others who were "advocating for our son's interests." We were directed to the "accused" chairs, which sat directly facing the judge, and in between the attorney seats. My husband, Ronald, Randie, and I took our places before the judge. The state's attorney sat closest to the judge. Daniel was assigned his own attorney, the Guardian ad litem (GAL), Wanda, who sat to our left. Randie sat to our right. To her right, a wall of CASA volunteers lined up in chairs against the wall. Before I sat down, the bailiff motioned to me with his finger. I had to place my coat and purse on his desk. I quietly complied with his request. I was the only woman in the court room not allowed to have my belongings by my side. As I returned to my seat, a wave of shame swept over me. I don't know why I felt shame in that moment, I hadn't done anything wrong. Perhaps it was because most everyone else present incorrectly surmised that we'd done the unthinkable. Hurt a child. A large invisible lens is placed directly in front of the "accused chairs." It is the abuse lens. Everyone looking through that lens views the case from the perspective that the people on the other side are perpetrators, incapable of caring appropriately for children. No-fault dependency cases are processed through juvenile court using the same protocols, procedures, and phraseology as neglect and abuse cases.

The judge entered the room. This was a Shelter Care hearing, which must be held within 48 hours when a child has been removed from his parents care, for whatever the reason. The judge looked at us with panic, fear, and disgust. She announced that it was a Shelter Care hearing and shouted at us, "I HAVE THE POWER TO TERMINATE YOUR PARENTAL RIGHTS!" We knew that she did. Another judge had done it to our adoptive son's birthmother in this very room.

Judicial Regrouping

All of the attorneys requested to meet with the judge in chambers. They left the room. We sat there quietly, fearful, not knowing what would happen. What seemed an eternity later, they re-entered the room and took their places. The judge announced that Daniel had serious psychiatric and psychological issues causing him to be a danger to himself and others and that we'd abandoned him at the psychiatric hospital at the advice of a therapist for our safety. She described the damage that he'd done to our house as "incalculable" and stated that it was one of the worst cases they'd ever seen. Agreeing with the attorneys, she concurred that Jim and I had gone above and beyond trying to help him. She asked Ronald a few questions. He supported our decision. A court order required Ronald to coordinate Daniel's therapies. The judge announced that there was cause to take him into temporary custody. She instructed us in a phrase that we would hear repeatedly over the next several years: "You must cooperate and comply with the terms of the service agreement or risk termination of parental rights." Of course, we would. She brought the gavel down. It was over. Or was it just beginning?

Tears of Reality

We re-entered the little room outside the courtroom. Briefly I spoke to Wanda, saying that I remembered her from years ago. She was the attorney for both of our adoptive sons when they were infants and toddlers. She didn't remember, nor did I expect that she would. It was a long time ago and she had over 300 cases annually. She responded by saying, "We had a case like this years ago, but the boy wasn't as bad as *your* son. He aged out of the system." The reality of what she said hit me like a ton of bricks. The reality of what might lie ahead. I couldn't hold it in anymore. The flood gates opened. I stood there and wept.

We met with Randie for coffee afterwards. She told us that the judge was outraged that no one had helped us. She had expressed her frustration, "Why didn't someone help this family?!" Randie commented further that the judge was sympathetic, empathetic, and aghast that there was no help to be found for us, short of doing this. They had reviewed the Juvenile Court Act to see if the case could be a dependency case from the start. They concluded from the statute that we had to be charged with neglect first. Once the state took custody, they could amend it to no fault dependency. Randie had advocated strongly for us. She had asked the judge if there was any way that the neglect charge would stick. The judge assured her that as long as we stayed active and involved, that would not be her intention.

Emotional Aftermath

That night, Ronald came to our home for his weekly visit. It was the first time he'd come to counsel us, rather than Daniel. We didn't even know where Daniel was. Ronald helped us work through our emotions which ranged from relieved to depressed and from worried to frightened. The session was interrupted by the phone ringing. It was Daniel. He was frantic. I asked him where he was. He said he was at a group home about an hour and a half away. "Are you ok?" we asked.

He said, "They told me you are in trouble, Mom. I don't want you in trouble trying to help me." I told him that we'd been to court and the judge understood the situation. We tried to assure him that everything would be all right and that he shouldn't worry. We'd be there to see him just as soon as we could. No one was telling him anything either. He didn't know if he could call us, so he marched right up to the staff and told them he was calling us anyway. They didn't stop him. He said that DCFS had interrogated him a couple of times, asking him if we'd abused him. Had we hit him? Had we left marks on him? Had we kicked him out of the house? Did he have drug or alcohol problems? Did we? Did we hit each other? "No, no," he replied. They pushed him further, "Are you sure? Are you sure they didn't abuse you?" Finally, he screamed at him, "I HAVE GOOD PARENTS! THEY NEVER HURT ME! THE PROBLEM IS WITH ME!"

Transition: Post Adopt to Case Management

Taking this step changed our family's status with DCFS. We were still a "Post-Adopt" family as we had one other child under that department's caseload. Concurrently, we now had another case open under DCFS Placement and Permanency. DCFS transitioned our youngest son, Daniel, from Post-Adopt to Case Management before our emotions had a chance to catch up.

Incongruously, there was emphasis on the very same word as the one they used when they took him out of foster care originally. Permanency. If permanency was so ultra-important before he got adopted, why was preserving that adoption not equally as important now? Why was there suddenly all this talk about his permanency goal? We didn't separate from him, nor he from us. In our eyes, we were still a family. The government had made him a legal orphan by their design, not ours.

On April 10, we received notice that our adoption subsidy for Daniel was stopped. How ironic that it took years and the drastic step of relinquishing custody to get funding for treatment, but a subsidy could be stopped on a dime. It made sense that the board payment would be withdrawn. We were no longer financially supporting him. It just seemed irreconcilable that while every other part of the system was deliberately slow, subsidy accounting was lightning fast. But, that wasn't all that we lost.

We also receive word from Ronald that his supervisor would not allow him to coordinate therapy for Daniel, citing we were no longer a "Post-Adopt" family. Apparently, they'd dismissed the notion that we had a second post adopt child. I reminded him that he was under court order to do so. His supervisor planned to notify the court that they would like to have someone else be appointed to provide services. In truth, they had a large contract with DCFS. Aligning with us in court placed them in direct opposition to DCFS. They notified us in writing that they feared losing their DCFS contract as a result of advocating alongside of us, for our son's much needed post-adopt trauma therapy. They withdrew from us. They kept their contract. We lost our only support system.

Reconnecting

On April 26, we were finally allowed to visit Daniel. The state had deprived us of seeing our son for almost a full month. We could now visit weekly, and did so, but it also meant 3 hours of travel each time we went. He gave bad reports of the group home. There were gang members there and a really bad sex offender. Some of the kids were taking drugs. Many were runaways. The kids were having sex in the closets. We wondered where the supervision was. He was afraid to sleep at night for fear of being raped.

Emotional Mend

Scrambled thoughts swirled around in my head. I kept thinking about how all the people who'd been involved in our lives, seemed to have a little different perspective, yet none of them fully comprehended the trauma we'd all been forced to live with. Having a child with severe emotional needs can be very isolating. Friends don't enjoy spending time with a child who quickly gets angry and disruptive. If anyone came close to getting it, it was Ronald and Dr. Lisa. I pondered some of the comments that were darting around in my mind.

One therapist—"Lighten up, quit walking on eggshells."

Therapeutic school—"He's fine here; the problems are at home. It's the parent's fault."

Ronald—You are looking at a lifetime of mental illness. He will not get better without you."

Residential therapist—"I don't know if we can get him stable, he needs to be in high end residential treatment facility. No one should have to put up with what you did. It's amazing you did it so long."

Wanda—"We had a case like this years ago, but he was not as bad as your son. He aged out of system."

A caseworker—"Daniel's problems are deep and scary."

A judge—"This is one of the worst cases I've seen."

A hospital therapist—"If you want mental health care, maybe you should move to Canada. You're not going to get it here."

I spent a Sunday afternoon cleaning his room, which was very dirty. I picked up the garbage and dirty laundry and vacuumed the carpet. I washed his bedding. I put his things away. I washed the walls and the window. I took down the window blinds which he'd smashed and threw them away. I made notes that we'd have to repair the holes in the walls, replace the closet door and fix the bedroom door. Jim asked if he could help me. No, it was something I needed to do myself. I cried the whole time. And there was the rest of the house to repair. A scratched mirror. The railing torn off the wall. Bent heater grates. More holes in the walls. Broken doors. We had so many keys for all the doors to stop him from breaking in to people's things; we didn't even know which keys corresponded to which doors. It would take a year to repair most of the damage.

Ronald said that repairing the house was symbolic of our emotional wounds, suggesting that as we repaired our home, we might also find emotional healing. We'd been emotionally beaten up by our son, whom we loved so much, and DCFS and the judicial system were about to beat us up some more.

Residential Placement

On April 29, the Child and Youth Investment Team (CAYIT) meeting commenced, a DCFS-led a meeting to talk about where Dan should be placed. They identified his biggest strength as having a strong and loving family and that he should be placed in a residential facility, in close proximity to our home. Their "team" would select two placements for us to interview. They'd let us choose between them. We had no say in this process, except to tell them what Daniel's strengths were.

On May 19, DCFS called and told us which places they selected. One was within five minutes of our home. Initially, we thought this might be our choice. We'd used some of their therapists before and they had not worked out, however their counseling center was the same one that had helped us appropriately diagnose Chip. I set up an interview. They had a concern and so did we. Their concern was that it was so close to our home, that if he were to go AWOL, he was likely to run home. We'd have to call the police to get him back there. Our concern was that they their program was focused on children with willful behavior. We were not convinced that they understood or could treat trauma. If we placed him here, he was likely to remain for the duration of his childhood and we didn't want that.

The second choice on their list was an hour away from our home. I interviewed them the very next day. They did not have an available bed, but thought that one might be opening up within the next few weeks. We discussed diagnoses and therapies at length. The admissions counselor was more than a little surprised that I was educated regarding specific trauma therapies, even fairly new ones. He agreed to help give our son trauma focused therapies, if we decided to place him there. I also knew that for Daniel, given the choices, this facility was at the bottom of his list. There was a psychiatric hospital next door to the residential building. The hospital was his first in-patient psychiatric placement. He hated it there. I recalled driving by the residential center in past months, with Daniel in the car, telling him how much I wanted him to work on therapy so that he didn't end up in the residential center. It was where kids lived, when their behaviors could not safely be managed at home. At the time, he dismissed my comments. We'd want to visit often. We were looking at a two hour commute every visit. Hopefully, it would be short term, long enough to get him stable enough to come home. He certainly had a better chance here than at the center closer to our home.

Daniel was visibly annoyed when the caseworker arrived the following day to remove him from the group home. His peers there had been teaching him about gang culture and how to manipulate his caseworker to get material things. They told him to tell her that his clothes were all too small and didn't fit. The other kids told him that DCFS would be happy to give him a large stipend for clothing. He was quite pleased with himself when his plan worked. He received more than $350 for new clothes. Since we had made sure he had seven new shirts and seven new pairs of jeans, as well as socks and underclothing, he spent his entire clothing stipend on expensive designer sneakers. Now that he was indoctrinated into gang culture, he desired to dress the part. Designer shoes were "cool" to this demographic of youth and he desired to rise to the top of their echelon. During his stay there, he'd decided that it wasn't so bad living with few rules and little accountability. He resigned to himself that he'd just stay there and "hang out." So, when his caseworker arrived to transport him and his designer shoes to the residential center, which just happened to be geographically adjacent to the one behavioral health hospital that he deplored, he was more than a little ticked off.

From that dreadful day of abandoning him at a psychiatric in-patient hospital to protect ourselves, the child/victim/perpetrator, had been bounced around to three different placements over the course of 51 days. He had traveled 10 miles from the hospital to a crisis center and stayed two days. Next, he traveled another 10 miles to a shelter and stayed for two more days. The caseworker arrived and transported him 40 miles away where he remained for 49 more days before traveling the final stretch of 40 miles to the residential treatment center. More than 100 miles later, he ended up within minutes of the original lockout site. From the vantage point of the behavioral health hospital where we'd left him, you could practically see the residential treatment center.

He ended up just five miles from where he started.

*"I have learned over the years
that when one's mind is made up,
this diminishes fear; knowing what
must be done does away with fear."*

Rosa Parks

"Feel the fear and do it anyway."

Dr. Susan Jeffers

Chapter Eight

FIGHTING BACK

ON JUNE 1, 2008, we received a notice from DCFS informing us that we'd been "indicated" in a child abuse investigation. As a result, our names had been placed on the state central register of "indicated perpetrators." The notice detailed information on how to file an appeal as well as the rule that DCFS had used to justify their finding. It was Rule #84, Lockout.

We had devoted our lives to children including those who were ours and those who weren't. We'd done our very best to take care of our severely mentally ill son. We'd been forced into locking him out because of lack of any other appropriate options. Somehow, under the law, this made us criminals. It was clear that the only issue at hand was that our son was mentally ill. We were vexed and embittered. It was a slap in the face.

We filed an appeal immediately.

In reading Lockout Rule #84, we quickly detected that the investigator had violated several of the provisions. Randie spoke to the DCFS Administrative Law Court attorney who was surprised and confused as to why DCFS had done this. The DCFS attorney suggested that we file an appeal. As long as the neglect charge was amended to no fault dependency, the ruling was likely to be in our favor and our names would be expunged from the child abuser list.

We immediately identified three criteria in which DCFS could not have indicated the finding against us, had they done due diligence in reading and reviewing their own rules. These criteria which *prevent* DCFS investigators from "indicating" findings against parents due to "lockout" include:

1. The child has a history of mental health problems
2. The child is dangerous towards family members
3. The family has had a clinical staffing

Since all three of those criteria applied to our case, they should have resolved the investigation with a finding of: "unfounded."

We returned to the juvenile court on July 10, 2008 for the Adjudication hearing. Daniel was found to be dependent upon the state of Illinois through no fault or lack of concern by his parents. The neglect finding was amended to no fault dependency. It was official. Our son was once again a ward of the state of Illinois, for the second time in his short 13 years of life; *a "second time" foster child.*

On July 16, 2008, Randie called the Administrative Law court to petition for our names to be expunged from the child abuser list. The Administrative Law Judge expunged the "indicated" finding and our names were removed from the state central register of "indicated perpetrators." Our names had already been removed before Randie called to petition for it. The judge thought what they had done to us was preposterous.

The School

In reading the investigative interviews, we discovered that the school principal gave a bad report about us to the DCFS investigator, which blamed us for our son's emotional issues and destruction at home. We sent a letter to the Superintendent of the Special Education Department to file a complaint against the principal of the therapeutic school. We wanted to alert her superiors that, unlike everyone else, she had not given us much needed support; instead, she chose to blame the parents. We never received a response from the school district.

DCFS Investigations

We also filed a complaint against the DCFS investigators with the Office of Investigator General (OIG) for breaking DCFS rules regarding Lockout Rule #84. In filing such a complaint, the parents are told that an investigation will ensue; however, results of the investigation would not be released. We'd never know if it was taken seriously; or so we thought. The results of our complaint were written in a report to the governor and state legislators in 2010, sans names. Enough details were written that there was no question that General Investigation #4 was the result of the Hoy complaint which was filed in 2008.

OIG uncovered a variety of mistakes that the investigators had made. Most notably, they never interviewed our son's regular psychiatrists and therapists; favoring instead to weigh heavily upon reports of a school principal, who blamed us rather than supported us, and in-patient hospital staff who barely knew our son. The investigators responded by saying they attempted to interview the psychiatrists and therapists, as required by the rule, but were unable to reach them. The report notes that DCFS records show no attempts to ever contact them.

Also, even after the charges were amended to no fault dependency, and the "indicated" finding was expunged, both the paper and electronic data files still showed that the case was a result of a "neglect" charge and that we remained on the state central register as "indicated perpetrators" as a result.

The Office of Investigator General recommended that DCFS Post Adopt and Advocacy be provided information on a Voluntary Placement Agreement for:

> "...situations where parents and guardians have reached the limits of their abilities to deal with children who exhibit extreme emotional, behavioral, medical or other issues, the option of entering into a voluntary placement agreement should be presented. **Voluntary placement agreements allow children to be moved to a placement while parents or guardians**

and professionals work towards reunification. During the course of this investigation, the OIG found the Department currently has no administrator assigned to oversee the voluntary placement agreement process and there is a lack of familiarity among other workers as to its availability or implementation. As voluntary placement agreements can be entered into to provide stability and prevent involvement with the Juvenile Court, their utilization should be formalized and encouraged throughout the Department."

The investigator and her supervisor received little more than a slap on the wrist. They were both given non-disciplinary counseling in proper administration of Lockout Rule #84. In private enterprise, if an employee blatantly violated company rules causing someone to face civil charges in court, *they would have been fired.*

The Office of Investigator General detailed five recommendations and responses as follows:

1. The Department should correct Department electronic records databases (CYCIS and SACWIS) screens to reflect that the family's case is open as a no-fault dependency, not neglect. The databases have been corrected.

2. The Department should draft a memo to be attached to the inside front cover of the file entitled "Error Correction" that explains the neglect finding was expunged. Suggested language: <u>The parents have not been indicated for neglect. The case is open as a result of a no-fault dependency. A copy of this Error Correction sheet should be included whenever copies of the file are made.</u> A memorandum has been placed in the file.

3. The Department's Clinical Division and the Post-Adoption Unit should be provided information on the use of voluntary placement agreements. The use of Voluntary Placement Agreements (VPA) was discussed with all clinical managers statewide. The issue of Voluntary Placement Agreements was also discussed at a Clinical All Team Meeting. Those in attendance included the regional nurses, clinical managers, clinical coordinators, sexual behavior problem

coordinators and clerical staff. An Information Transmittal regarding the use of Voluntary Placement Agreements was also distributed.

4. The Department should pursue non-disciplinary counseling of the child protection investigator **for failing to interview the attending psychiatrist at the psychiatric hospital, the boy's treating psychiatrist and his treating therapist.** Counseling should include a review of the factors to be considered in a lockout investigation as cited in this report.

5. The Department should pursue non-disciplinary counseling of the child protection investigator's supervisor for **failing to ensure Department Procedures 300, Reports of Child Abuse and Neglect, Appendix B, Allegation: Lock-Out was followed.** The supervisor was counseled.

While expressing my frustration to a case management supervisor about this blatant violation of investigator rules, the supervisor responded by saying, "Look, somewhere along the way, every foster parent gets 'vilified.' Get over it!"

Post-Adopt and Clinical had failed us. We had fought them and lost. Investigations had criminalized us. We had fought them and won. Soon after, we also had to fight a court appointed volunteer, which I expand upon in Chapter 11.

"Alone we can do so little; together we can do so much."

Helen Keller

"The greatest of faults, I should say, is to be conscious of none."

Thomas Carlyle

Chapter Nine

LACK OF SYNERGY

LIKE SARAH PALIN, I TOO, was a hockey mom. During all those years that I schlepped a van full of hockey gear from rink to rink, I learned a new word as I sat watching all those hockey practices. "Synergy." The sum of the parts is greater than the whole. Anything synergized manifests positively on the back side, including how state departments interface with each other.

The child welfare system compounds and perpetuates itself because the departments within "the Department," as they like to call themselves, work separately from one another. Four separate departments within the Illinois Department of Children and Family Services are involved in a post-adopt child psychiatric lockout case. They include Post Adopt, Clinical, Investigations, and Case Management. As the family moves from one to the next, there is virtually no communication between them. Each department scrutinizes the parents and child in their own way, with the magnifying lens reaching its greatest degree of dissection at the case management level. While Post-Adopt does not factor scope and the long term effects of failure to provide intensive services, the other three departments have their own custom made forms of the "abuse lens."

Post-Adopt or Adoption Preservation Programs came about largely because of the Adoptive and Safe Families Act of 1997 (ASFA). I will explain the benefits and deficits of this federal law in Chapter 15, but for now, suffice it to say that it was former President Clinton's way of getting large numbers of foster children into permanent homes via adoption. Unfortunately, his vision didn't extend past adoption through to adoption preservation. The ultimate cost to this short sighted bill has resulted in adoption disruption and dissolution, creating second time foster children.

Post-Adopt Benefits

As a parent who utilized many of the Post-Adopt services, it's important to acknowledge the array of services that DCFS Post-Adopt does offer parents. These services include counseling, educational assistance, a Medicaid card, and financial assistance.

DCFS contracts with various providers throughout the state that offer child and family counseling to help parents obtain services for a variety of issues including child development, chronic behavior, trauma, and adoption. These services are provided to the families at no cost in order to prevent adoption disruption and dissolution, thus preserving the adoption.

Another helpful service that we used, as needed, was the DCFS educational liaisons. Adoptive parents may call on these caseworkers who work in tandem with school professionals, parents and children, to help them navigate the special educational issues that inherently manifest with child plagued by trauma issues. In our experience, the DCFS educational liaisons were top notch and one of the most helpful components of our child's treatment team. They offered insight and direction that others didn't provide. For children who need medical services and devices, DCFS Post-Adopt can often be helpful in getting approval for specialized items that a Post-Adopt child needs such as cochlear implants, walkers, and other specialized medical equipment. For families that don't need any of those services, but feel the effects of increased financial hardship due to excessive transportation costs for medical appointments and other meetings, Post-Adopt may offer increased subsidy board payments to aid the family in meeting their child's needs. For a child like our son, Chip, this array of services was sufficient to stabilize his condition and allow him to safely remain living in our home. For children like Daniel, whose conditions cause them to be too aggressive and violent to remain safely in a family setting, the available services fall short.

Post-Adopt Deficits

The largest deficit of the DCFS Post-Adopt program in Illinois is that they allow the children with the most critical needs to fall through the cracks. They fail to monitor families in crisis, neglect to track repeated child psychiatric hospitalizations, and don't catch families before the bottom falls out completely.

Red Flag

Repeated calls and contacts to the subsidy worker signal a red flag that a family is in crisis and in need of personal case management. While the red flag lay on the subsidy caseworker's desk for months or years, DCFS fails to raise it until it is too late to preserve the family.

The subsidy workers offer the usual array of counseling, referrals, and subsidy increase while reiterating that residential treatment is not included in the continuum of services. They fail to alert the Clinical Department that serious trouble is imminent. It is only once the red flag has been raised, that the subsidy worker informs the family that they may request a DCFS clinical staffing, which may already be too late. Often, better resources for parents include other parents who have successfully navigated the system or a good special education attorney. However, many families are unable to afford attorneys, even those who charge modest fees.

By raising the red flag earlier and offering early monitoring and intervention at the family's request, the family is more likely to receive the appropriate services, decreasing the possibility of escalated crisis intervention later on.

DCFS Clinical

In retrospect, I'm cynical regarding DCFS' true commitment to adoption preservation. To allow even one child to be relinquished back into the system to access mental healthcare, defeats the entire purpose in having a large department specifically dedicated to its purpose. I have long wondered why DCFS caseworkers accept agendas that prohibit adoption preservation such as obscuring helpful protocols, dependency coaching, and failing to provide guidance and support.

The DCFS Clinical Department can be helpful to families if the family is aware that they have a protocol which helps. Herein lies the problem. The fact that this track even exists is hidden. Subsidy workers and adoption preservation specialists only reveal this track when the family is out of options. To be effective, it should happen much earlier. If the family actually discovers that there is a clinical division, getting an appointment with a clinical caseworker is no small task. It's not impossible; it just takes a long time. For us, it equated to a six week long wait, several wrong caseworker volleys, a whole lot of phone call begging, and two more crises replete with in-patient hospitalizations. Once the date is penciled in on the calendar, the family is holding its breath that the sky doesn't completely cave in before the day arrives. The appointment schedulers fail to inform the family of the agenda protocol, thus the family arrives with false expectations and at the close of the staffing; they will leave without anything that even resembles a solution. When the clinical division also fails to successfully help the family, some DCFS clinicians are misleading parents into thinking that filing a dependency petition will be helpful to them.

At times, not even DCFS Clinical can help the family. Clinicians may be familiar with the long standing protocol of dependency petitions; however they fail to inform families of the tragedy that lies ahead for them and their child. Either the clinicians are not aware of the events which follow, or they make a conscious choice not to disclose them. Clinicians coach parents that the only option they have left is to abandon their child at the psychiatric hospital and file a dependency petition in juvenile court. Regardless of the reason for their advice, parents enter juvenile court being ill prepared for what they face. Clinicians have little or no communication with departments within their own organization, which take the family through the next few phases. Investigators proceed as if it is a run-of-the-mill abuse investigation, failing to factor the family's long standing attempts at attaining funding for residential care. Favoring instead, to scrutinize parents through their own personal abuse lenses before handing them off to the Permanency and Placement Department. Lack of communication and synergy between the Clinical and Investigation departments unwittingly propel families into an investigation with neglect or abuse bias.

To describe our experience, towards the end of our clinical staffing, Jean asked if we would be picking our son up from the hospital. Realizing that we could not do that and still maintain safety in our home, the discussion took on a completely different tone. She stated that she would be recommending residential treatment for our son. That statement was preceded by mild verbal threats which indicated that she had some suspicion that we were "dumping" our son back onto the system because we didn't want to deal with normal teen problems. She cautioned us that we'd better stay involved in his care and we'd "better visit him and work towards bringing him home." She seemed to have some sense that we wished to be relieved of our parenting responsibilities. This seemed such a preposterous notion to me considering we have four children which span five years apart in age. Daniel is the youngest, and he was 13 years old at the time of the staffing. We were full blown into the teen years with all four kids. The older three children were doing great despite normal teen issues, coupled with the fact that we were living with their brother, who was causing us all to live in terror. If that wasn't a recipe for teen disaster, I failed to see what was. Obviously, we were well equipped to deal with normal teen issues. However we were there to admit that we were out of our league in dealing with a severe emotional disorder. We haven't spent a decade doing therapy with our child for naught. Jean hadn't pulled out the jumbo size "abuse lens", but she was certainly wearing the "abuse bifocals."

DCFS Investigations

The lack of synergy ignites a stream of problems relative to DCFS Investigations; including bias against parents, verbal threats, unnecessary child and sibling interrogations, hasty interviews, and lack of adhesion to lockout rules.

When DCFS Investigations is assigned to a psychiatric lockout case, they are not necessarily clued in on all the details from the start. They just know that a child has been abandoned at a psychiatric hospital. Since the numbers of true neglect and abuse cases far outweigh the psychiatric lockout cases, an investigator mindset is likely already weighing towards guilty. Illinois investigators are instructed to "err on the side of the child." In fact, 75% of child abuse and neglect investigations, which are closed with an "indicated" finding are later overturned on appeal in Administrative Law Court. This statistic was proven in the Illinois Supreme Court case won by Chicago's Family Defense Center, DuPuy vs. Samuels. In addition, I attended a public meeting in which a DCFS Investigations Administrator openly admitted, that investigators readily "indicate" findings based upon the credibility of the hotline caller, especially if the caller was a police officer or from a school or hospital. After the meeting, when questioned, she clarified her position on the issue by saying that "indicated findings" are not automatic based upon the hotline caller; however, a call reported by a community professional has greater weight than other random callers. Unfortunately, their perspective fares poorly for parents facing a psychiatric lockout, who are likely to be indicated because the hotline call generates from a mental health hospital.

Investigators sometimes utilize scare tactics when interviewing families, threatening to remove their children from their home if they do not cooperate or answer every question. Cooperation is loosely defined as anything that the investigator wants them to do or say. Parents cave in to their fears and relinquish rights, unlike they would do in any other setting. Parents must agree to whatever safety plan the investigator issues, take whatever classes they are assigned, and subject themselves to scrutiny.

Concurrently, investigators interview the siblings of the locked out child. Sometimes interviews take place in the family's home in the presence of their parents or attorney. However, investigators are known to enter school buildings and make a request to school officials that siblings be removed from their classrooms, for questioning in a private room. Investigators may scare children, as they may have no clue as to why they are being questioned.

They ask questions repeatedly, confusing them and leaving them wondering if the investigator will go away if they could only figure out what answer they were expecting to hear. Children want to please adults and may say whatever they think the investigator wants to hear, just to end the interview.

Finally, the child who was locked out is also caught off guard and subsequently interviewed. The investigator fails to consider that there was no neglect or abuse at all to begin with, just a state system of care that has a giant gaping hole in it. Thus, the child is interviewed in exactly the same manner as a child who was alleged to have been neglected or abused. Akin to the sibling interview, investigators repeat questions over and over. What makes this interview inherently more harrowing than an ordinary investigation is that this child is already dealing with a severe mental illness and emotional disregulation. The child feels separation and abandonment, rather than the love and support from his family, which compounds the situation. Telling the child his parents are "in trouble," as they did to our son, increases his anxiety and insecurity levels incrementally.

There are a few problems inherent with the investigation process itself. While the investigator is charged with interviewing everyone who comes in regular contact with the child, he also has a time constraint for doing so. It is difficult, if not impossible to gauge a parent's relationship to a child in the space of a 45 minute interview. Also, they have a tendency to hang on the worst information, not defining it within the context in which it was delivered. Then of course, there is everyone's busy schedule to jockey around and some interviews are missed all together. That by itself is not necessarily an issue, but the risk is that one or two phrases are likely to make it into the report, skewing the interview against the parents.

Investigators either don't always know their own organizational rules, or simply don't follow them. This happened in our case when the Office of Investigator General investigated them and discovered they were not well versed in Lockout Rule #84.

About a year later, another set of parents, who were facing a psychiatric lockout, contacted me. I prepared them for the investigation, so they'd know what to expect, and to help them protect themselves in court. I suggested that they print out the DCFS Lockout rules, so that they could highlight to the investigator, the reasons they could not be indicated, if he should threaten to do so. The investigator was rude and belligerent, and did threaten to place their names on the State Central Register of child abusers. The parents showed the investigator three places in Rule #84 which proved that he was not allowed to do so. The parents attended a DCFS clinical staffing, their son had severe, documented mental health issues, and he was dangerous towards his family. The investigator boldly stated that he intended to defy DCFS rules and indicate the finding against them anyway. He followed through and did so.

As an independent insurance agent, I have a hard time with investigators not knowing their rules. I sell for many different insurance companies. It is impossible to memorize all the guidelines, all the endorsements, and all the policies for each company. The human brain simply cannot encompass it all. So, I commonly remember basic policies and common endorsements for each company. However, when I get the small house with the six car garage, one of kind family heirloom, and the car that no insurance company wants to insure; that's when I start reading and re-reading policies to make sure I have all my bases covered. Many investigators not only rush through the process, they don't go back and read their own rules. The majority thinking is that if there is an avenue to indicate the finding against the parents, that's the way it trends. If the parents are interested in clearing their names, they can always appeal. It really works pretty well for the investigator. If they overlook something and a child dies, they are on the hook with the government. If they accuse almost everyone, they have at least a 25% chance of being right, leaving the other 75% to hire an attorney and fight it on appeal.

Once the case has been closed as "indicated" or "unfounded," the investigators pass the abuse lens to the case workers.

Case Management

Virtually all cases are approached as if the parents are abusive or neglectful, even if the case was subsequently amended to no fault dependency. This is in part, due to the fact that the case management and legal procedures for neglect, abuse, and dependency are one and the same. Rather than treat the case on its own merits, investigators mirror the same procedures and protocols as abuse cases. Why? Because no other track currently exists within the system.

Setting Goals

The caseworker is charged with setting goals to move the case along. This includes goals for the child; which in this case include therapeutic goals and family reunification. Essentially, it is everything the child is charged with doing to navigate his way safely back into his bedroom in his family home. The case plan outlines the types of therapies, the frequency of therapy, academic goals, behavior goals, and evidence of emotional stabilization. The case plan also includes goals for the family.

What goals could be set for a family for which there is no neglect or abuse, but simply lacks the ability to manage a mentally or emotionally unsafe child within their family structure? I can speak only for our family in stating that our goals were pretty simple. DCFS had to know our phone number and address and we had to participate in family therapy if we were asked. Perhaps that sounds reasonable to you, unless you consider that we'd had the same phone number and address for over 17 years, which didn't exactly set the stage for a flight risk. Regarding family therapy, since we have not one, but two sons with mental illness, family therapy had been a way of life for the entire 11 years they'd been living in our home. Apparently, we'd been compliant before we knew we needed to be. The caseworker explained it by saying she was required to assign some type of goal. She had other duties as well, including monitoring us with monthly interviews and home inspections.

Meetings

Annually, there are two types of meetings the parent must attend relative to a no fault dependency case, meetings that have to do with stabilizing the child's mental health condition, and others that have to do with monitoring the parents. Those that have to do with stabilizing the child's mental health are multiple clinical staffings and school meetings. All of the rest serve to examine the parents through the abuse lens.

The clinical staffing meetings have everything to do with your child. They consist of you, your child, and your child's treatment team. It's important for your child to be at these because it's important that he be vested in the process of making progress. It's a time of looking back at where he was, taking stock of where he needs to be, and everyone being on the same page to make sure he gets there. These are generally held 4 times per year. The second type of meeting pertains to the school. There are IEP (Individualized Educational Plan) and other school meetings, which are held at least twice annually. Generally, you and your child meet with school officials to assess academic and social progress. Meetings are sometimes held at various intervals to address concerns or to change goals or placement plans. I found all these meetings helpful and was glad to attend them because I knew everyone wanted to help my son. However, the rest of the meetings seemed to have less to do with him, and more to do with us. Let's tally how many meetings per year a parent with a psychiatric lockout case attends.

School Staffings—2
Clinical staffings—4
Required meeting total—6

Chronologically, I'll discuss the rest of the meetings that occur from least to most often, starting and ending with meetings for the court's purposes. Prior to court, DCFS hosts a meeting called an Administrative Case Review, (ACR) which includes everyone involved except the school personnel. A DCFS reviewer schedules two meetings per year to go over the child's case from A-Z with the goal of making sure the case is moving along. This includes social, emotional, physical, and academic reviews and the child's treatment goals. It's a chance to update records, make corrections, and plan for reunification. This is also the court's record, so they have a synopsis of what transpired prior to the last court date. I'll add two more to the previous tally.

Administrative Case Reviews—2
Required meeting total—8

The other meetings in relation to the child are juvenile court hearings, which I describe in more detail in the following chapter. There are always at least 2 court hearings, but almost always there are more. Since there are a minimum of two, I'll add two more to the tally.

Court Hearings—2
Required meeting total—10

The following meetings listed, have only to do with monitoring parents. The caseworker is required to visit the parent's home monthly, evaluating the parent's progress, and inspecting their home. By this time, the DCFS caseworker has forgotten that when the child on his case was living in the home, the home was very unsafe, and DCFS refused to help. Now that the unsafe child has been clinically and residentially placed, and the home is safe, the worker is required to inspect the same home, overlooking the fact that the same environment is now safe, with absolutely no risk of physical or emotional harm to anyone.

An interview the caseworkers must conduct at certain intervals is called a CERAP or Child Endangerment Assessment Protocol. The CERAP was designed to evaluate the likelihood of immediate harm of a moderate to severe nature to a child victim, at several specific milestones throughout the life of a case. In the case of a psychiatric lockout/no fault dependency case, the system identifies the locked out child as a child *victim*, when in reality, the child is the *perpetrator*. The *true victims* are the child's siblings and likely his parents or any other family members living in the home. DCFS routinely completes the CERAP form on the safe child rather than the unsafe children!

The CERAP is a 14 question "yes or no" survey which indicates the presence of or absence of safety risk factors, complete with home inspection. The caseworker completes the CERAP as if the locked out child was abused, when in fact; he was the one causing the abuse to everyone else. It was unnerving to have every family member be interrogated regarding Daniel's safety when each of us had been physically hurt by him at one point or another. Perhaps they should have been equally as concerned when we were denied assistance for his treatment. CERAP fails to serve a useful purpose in a no fault dependency case. We never found any consistency regarding the frequency of CERAPs. Some of the caseworkers did them only before court and others insisted upon them monthly. They may do them monthly if they choose, thus we'll add 12 more to the tally.

Parent home inspection, CERAP, and interview–12
Required meeting total–22

Immediately after the clinical staffing, the caseworker would conduct the Child Family Team meetings. As they were a repeat of the staffing just held, they were often a waste of time.

Child-Family Team Meetings–4
Required meeting total–26

The judge has the liberty to appoint CASA or not. If they are appointed, they are required to "visit" your child monthly. They may also "visit" the parents alone, or continue dehumanizing them by requiring that they "observe a visit" between them and their child. I challenge you to envision parents of a child with leukemia taking their child to a chemotherapy session, only to be met by a court appointed volunteer, who requires them to be subjected to being supervised and evaluated while they visit their child. Dealing emotionally with such an appointment is traumatizing enough for parents of any chronically sick child. However, the stigma of a mentally ill child is pervasive and misunderstood. The family is required to tolerate the visits or risk termination of rights. We swallowed them like bad medicine and masked the indignity as best we were able. The system as a whole accepts and encourages these visits as if the parents were incapable of representing their child's "best interests." Add 12 more to the tally.

CASA visits–12

Required meeting total–38
Total meetings to stabilize the child – 6
Total meetings to monitor the family of a mentally ill child – 32+

The child gets his fair share of personal meetings which take place without the loving support of his parents. Add 2 more for the child to be interviewed prior to court hearings by the GAL, his state paid attorney. He'd endure at least 12–24 more interviews by the caseworker; all in which he is questioned if his parents are safe towards him. Add 12 more for CASA to ask more of the same, protecting the child's interests in lieu of his parents.

The tally is a minimum number, provided there are no extenuating circumstances of problems, but with mental health issues, there always are. Parents forced into no fault dependency cases can expect to attend a meeting of one sort or another almost weekly. At risk of being labeled uncooperative and losing the rest of our parental rights, we made every oppressive one of them. Eventually, we expected to be criticized, observed, monitored, evaluated, scrutinized, questioned, interrogated, investigated, humiliated, degraded, and dehumanized. And just when it seemed one person put down the abuse lens, someone else came along and grabbed it again. In the weeks prior to our semi-annual treks to juvenile court, we'd have to endure several of these meetings in the space of a week or two.

As court dates loomed, we endured the CASA visit, the caseworker visit, the clinical staffing, the child-family team meeting, the ACR, and court in a span of a couple of weeks. On our family calendar, we designated every March and September, "Hell Month."

Seen as Abusive

The entire process felt vicariously like it must have been for their birth mother, so long ago. There were too many meetings, too many demands, too many criticisms. The acronyms hadn't changed either, ACR, CAYIT, SACWIS, CERAP, CANTS, GAL. The paperwork and procedure was all the same, and so was the phraseology. "You must cooperate, comply with the terms of the service agreement, or risk termination of parental rights. You must make progress towards your goals." We would hear this phrase over and over again. It was about the usual thing. What we really needed was the right thing.

Could we really blame the caseworkers? Yes and no. Periodically, we'd tire of all the put-downs and inquire if they could just treat it on its own merits. Sometimes they'd answer that they just forgot. They didn't really have too many of these kinds of cases. It wasn't the usual thing. They'd remind us that court was not about us, it was all about the child. They'd complain that they had too many cases. They were in a hurry. Ours was easy, just get it over with. It wasn't about the successes we'd had in parenting an emotionally disregulated child. It was about who the caseworkers and others perceived as a failure—us. We were judged all the time. As we sat in the accused seats in court—it seemed to us—very much about us.

Irony

Throughout, there was just one thing that didn't make sense to me, no matter how busy they all were. "Permanency." In juvenile court, it's all about the permanency goal. Setting that goal was the whole reason everyone was there in the first place. What was the goal? Return home? Independent living? Adoption? The very same people who had taken the child out of the foster care system the first time, were placing him back into the very same system to access mental healthcare, never so much as raising an eyebrow. As much as juvenile court was all about the child, did any one of them stop, even for a moment, to consider the ramifications for the child when taking away his original permanency goal? Did any of them ever lose sleep at night over it, as I was doing on a regular basis? The only thing worse than being abandoned the first time, is being abandoned the second time.

Did it ever occur to any of them that they'd defeated the original purpose?

If it ever bothered any of them at all, even for a fleeting second, not one of them ever mentioned it to me.

Chapter Ten

THE JUVENILE COURT RESPONSE

THE JUDGE DONS HIS ROBES and sits on his bench before a case in which there is no criminal, no crime, and no existing laws to apply to the parents sitting before him. The parents are stigmatized as bad parents as the case progresses through juvenile court, slating the child against his parents.

A psychiatric lockout case defaults to juvenile court in quick succession to a hotline call and child abuse investigation. According to the Illinois State Bar Association, "the court's main purpose is to help families and protect their children." Does the court, as a whole, succeed in this purpose relative to a psychiatric lockout situation?

Helping Families?

Does juvenile court help families in a psychiatric lockout case? In some ways, yes, it does. The court will make sure your child gets the therapeutic treatment he needs. The court also makes sure you visit your child, monitors the situation, and makes sure all the laws are being followed. The judge listens to every party before making an objective legal decision. However, the help that the juvenile court provides comes with a price for the child and his family. Continuing legal fees prohibit many families from getting good defense and a fair shake in court, but the bigger price takes its toll on the child and family's emotional state, as well as their relationships with each other. The court pits the child and his attorney in direct opposition to his parents and their attorney. This is never a good thing, when the only real issue is that a child requires intensive clinical needs. The child might see this as an opportunity to manipulate all these new adults for material gain or other benefits. The child who needs accountability the most, gets it the least. The adults don't always communicate with each other, so the child may further manipulate by playing one adult off of another.

Another area in which parents pay a price occurs when they are unnecessarily charged with neglect and stripped of some of their parental rights, especially guardianship. The court allows many other people to speak on behalf of their child's interests in place of his parents, who love and know the child best. Since so many other people are reporting to the judge regarding the child's well-being, the judge rarely, if ever allows the parents to speak. If parents do get a chance to speak in court, they are always last.

Does the benefit of treatment outweigh the cost to the child's mental health needs and his relationship to the people who love him the most?

Benefits of Juvenile Court
- Secure treatment
- Legal Oversight
- Objective Oversight

Deficits of Juvenile Court
- Child vs. parents
- Child manipulates
- Child less accountable
- Legal fees for state and family
- Wounded child/family relationship
- Parents charged with neglect
- Civil rights stripped for healthcare

Protecting Children?

Does juvenile court protect children? The answer to this question differs based upon whether we answer it in relation to child protection prior to, or after the lockout occurred.

If a mental illness causes your child to be violent and aggressive, his siblings are not safe. Since your child is in school and other community settings on a regular basis, other children within the community are unsafe as well. If your child has suicidal tendencies, he is not safe from himself. The juvenile court has no provision to protect a child or family against a mentally ill, unsafe child, so it is easy to conclude, that prior to a psychiatric lockout the juvenile court fails to protect children from a mentally ill, violent child.

When a family fails to obtain treatment for their child, and therapists are recommending a lockout for safety reasons; is everyone safe then? The locked out child gets therapy; so he is safe. The child no longer resides in the home or community; so they are safe. Once again, the costs include: a child going up against his parents in court, a child who manipulates and lacks accountability, unnecessary cost to the state and the family, wounded family relationships, and loss of parental civil rights.

Juvenile Court Act

Why does the court use the Juvenile Court Act to respond to such a case? Because there aren't any other laws on the books that even come close to addressing a child with severe clinical needs. In our experience, the judges were often as frustrated as we were. It sometimes seemed they were grabbing onto parts of laws trying to get some assembly of the round peg into the square hole. The task of navigating a path that has yet to be carved out is difficult for everyone.

Neglect vs. No Fault Dependency

When a parent has devoted virtually every waking moment to his child's therapeutic needs and maintaining family safety, it is unconscionable to consider that a parent would be charged with neglect. However, that is the prevailing charge against parents in these cases. The Juvenile Court Act addresses children who are abused, neglected, and dependent upon the court. Since there is no neglect or abuse, the general assumption is that the child falls under dependency; however, the Juvenile Court Act holds a provision which counters this assumption.

At the time of this writing, the Juvenile Court Act states that a child may not be found dependent solely for medical or financial need. This is interpreted by some courts that parents must be charged with neglect prior to having the case amended to "no-fault dependency." I use the word *some* courts because there is no consistency across the state regarding whether a psychiatric lockout case can enter the juvenile court system as a dependency case at the onset. I am not aware of any cases which started as dependency. Parents are charged with neglect at the start of the case. Some courts will amend the charge to "no-fault dependency" at the adjudicatory hearing, which is the time that the child actually becomes a ward of the state, while others deny parents this option. The judges, states' attorneys, guardian ad litems, parent's attorneys, and caseworkers, all interpret the law differently because it was intended for acts of abuse and neglect, rather than accessing clinical treatment.

Permanency

Every case that enters Juvenile Court is different from the one before it. What binds them together is that regardless of the circumstances that brought them there, every case is traumatizing for the child and the family. Regardless of the role in court, everyone agrees that the best place for a child is living in a family. The judge and DCFS bear the responsibility for moving the case along so that the child achieves permanency as quickly as possible.

While considering lockout cases, as in an abuse or neglect case, court personnel place a huge emphasis on permanency. Every court hearing brings conversation about the child's best interests and where he should be living. What separates a lockout dependency case is that the child already has permanency. He has a home, a family, and a place to dwell once he's stable enough to return to the family home. Child welfare and juvenile court create separation that didn't exist prior to the lockout. They break the family apart, treat and heal the child, and then attempt to reunify the family. In essence, what should be happening is that because of the emotional stress on both child and parent, system workers should really be doing their best to keep the child as connected to his family as possible. We often said, "We need *less* involvement and *less* interference, not *more*." In their quest to fill in their blanks and meet their deadlines, they'd forget that this was not just a poor, lonely child, who had a bad family or no family to call his own, but rather a very sick child, who'd lost a large part of the family who did love him in exchange for a chance at getting better. Most often it fell on deaf ears. Most of the time, family separation is a perceived threat, but there is a legal threat as well.

ASFA

The Adoptive and Safe Families Act of 1997 holds a provision that says if a child is in care 15 of 22 months, the court may move to sever the parent's rights. However, there are a couple of exceptions to this part of the law. The judge can elect not to sever the parent's rights, if he feels it is not is the child's best interests or if the family has not been provided helpful services. This would appear to be the situation for a lockout case. However, the stigma and misconceptions of associated court personnel may put even a victim of a psychiatric lockout at risk of permanent family dissolution. In our family's situation, the culprit was CASA, but it could easily have been another foster parent, a caseworker, GAL, the state's attorney, or even a judge. It has been one of those people, in other families' cases, that we personally know.

Administrative Law Court

Besides defending themselves in Juvenile Court, parents are often forced to fight in a second court, Administrative Law Court.

If DCFS has violated Lockout Rule #84 and indicated neglect charges against the parents, their names are placed on the State Central Register of Indicated Perpetrators for 5 years. The only way to remove them is to file a service appeal with the Administrative Law Court. Parents only have 45 days to file this appeal. It can be easy to overlook this time frame when dealing with the emotional turmoil brought about by an unwarranted child abuse investigation and unfamiliarity with the judicial system, as a whole.

Usually, the Administrative Law judge is amenable to deleting the parents' names from the list, as long as the charge in Juvenile Court is amended to "no-fault dependency." This is a quandary for the parent who was unable to get his neglect charge amended to "no-fault dependency," and whose name will be stuck on the list for 5 years. Fighting the administrative charge takes additional emotional and financial toll on the parents. The added stress and strain takes away valuable time and energy that could be spent working with their child's treatment team.

Child Rights and Parental Responsibility

The judge may or may not require the child to appear in court. Generally, judges like the child to be in court because the whole court experience is about him. The caseworker may recommend that he not be in court, due to emotional instability. The judge has the authority to overrule that decision. Children who can't emotionally handle normal daily activities, including school and peer relationships, certainly can't withstand the intimidating atmosphere of court. Regardless of whether or not the child attends the hearing, the judge wants to know the wishes and desires of the child. If the child is not mandated to appear in court, professionals other than his parents are mandated to speak on his behalf. The judge also wants to know the wishes and desires of the parents. Often the parent's wishes are overshadowed by sympathy for the child's wishes.

There are two problems with the child expressing his wishes to the court. Children are too immature to have foresight and they use adults who don't know them well, to manipulate the system.

Many children don't think past the here and the now. Impulsive decisions are common amongst children with attention deficit disorder, anxiety, obsessive compulsive disorder, and other emotional disorders. An adoptive or abused child may have a chronological age of 13, and yet be functioning emotionally as a 5 year old, and socially as an older teen or adult. He is happy to have some decision making ability separate from his parents, yet he lacks the life experience and foresight to make good decisions on his own. In addition, numerous new adults have entered his life. This spells opportunity for the child who finds it easy to manipulate all the new adults in his life, who are deceived by his manipulation, unlike his parents who are more savvy to his tricks.

While it is important that the child's wishes be expressed, unless the therapist and other treatment team members value the parents input, the parent's influence may be overridden by the child's personal desires, whether they are healthy and appropriate or not. Parents play a vital role in raising children to be mature, responsible adults. Children need loving guidance during the formative years so they build character which forms the base for success in adult life. When a child reaches a certain level of intelligence, he may discover his own rights which include refusal to take the medicine which is needed to stabilize his moods and behaviors. Even worse, other adults allow the child to manipulate and get into trouble and still hold the parents responsible for his behavior.

Child vs. Parents

When presented with the opportunity to attend a seminar on adult mental health courts, I took advantage of the opportunity to learn more about mental health and court. The adult mental health court personnel acknowledge that they need to improve the current system. While I don't agree with all their procedures, there is one component I like a lot-the idea that everyone in court is on the same page.

The state's attorney and the alleged criminal's attorney agree that the criminal behavior occurred as a result of mental illness. Together, the three of them put together a plan that helps the accused get his life back on track, which may include regular reporting, drug testing, classes, and other forms of rehabilitation. The accused avoids jail time in exchange for successfully completing the program.

In Illinois, there are no mental health courts for children. Unlike the adult mental health courts, the two sides are not only distinct; they are solidly on opposing sides. It's the child versus his parents. The child is the plaintiff and the parents are the defendants. The GAL makes this clear when he refers to your child as "my client." CASA makes this clear when he refers to your child as "my CASA child." Even the caseworker claims your child as, "my child." The judge makes it clear every time he announces in open court that he has the power to terminate your parental rights. While the issue is merely clinical, where the parents should have the same rights as a physically ill child, they stand in a courtroom in a face-to-face standoff with their mentally ill child, defending their parental rights.

In subsequent chapters, I discuss in greater detail the emotional turmoil this places on the child and his parents. Court personnel overpower parental authority causing stigma against parents, resulting systematic oppression.

Stigma

The first assistant state's attorney spoke to us shortly before the Shelter Care hearing. He told us that dependency petitions carry the same stigma as an abuse case. We made the mistake of thinking that as they got to know us, over time, the stigma would subside. We were wrong. Even when we were able to get them to see the case on its own merit, it wasn't long before one of the parties was replaced by someone else and we found ourselves right back in the "abuse box."

There were a number of things that made us feel oppressed, beginning with the general atmosphere in the court lobby. As with all court rooms, we expected to go through a metal detector. We didn't expect we couldn't have a cell phone with a camera, though, while caseworkers, attorneys, and others were allowed to keep theirs.

CASA, proudly displaying their colorful CASA monogrammed lanyards around their necks, would be milling around the lobby or congregating in front of their office which sat between both court rooms. When our name was called, not only did the assigned volunteer enter the court room, but their peers herded in behind them. They'd be laughing and giggling and asking each other if they were "going in," as if they were waiting in line at an amusement park. Sometimes volunteer trainees sat in and sometimes a CASA manager accompanied the one assigned, but often hoards of them entered, sitting in on our personal business for no valid reason. A few times there were others already in the court room and we never introduced to them or discovered who they were at all. As the hearing progresses, everyone speaks but the parents. The conversations revolve around how the child is doing, but are strongly overcast by discussions about the parent's progress, efforts, and willingness to cooperate, as if the parents were the ones who'd damaged property and hurt people. Maybe, just maybe, the judge might ask if the parents have anything to say as he swirls his chair around to exit the court room.

After appearing in court the first time, I implemented coping strategies to deal with the distress it caused me. I left my cell phone in the car and avoided jewelry and anything that might set off the metal detector. I placed only four items into my hands to take into the court room. I took a pad of paper, a pen, my car keys, and my eyeglasses. I left my purse in the car. I left my coat in the car too, even when it was cold. I learned to sit in my chair silently and take notes about who was there and what was said. And I made hash marks on my paper. One for every time they asked if I was cooperating, complying, making progress towards my goals, visiting my child, doing what I was told, etc. I penned one mark for every put-down. I'd leave without speaking to anyone but Randie. When we got outside, Jim would look at the hash marks and ask, "How many?" Every time I left, I was depressed for a little while. It was good to go to work afterwards and get to spend the afternoon with people who were pleasant to be around and who valued my presence and intelligence.

Winters in the Chicago area get pretty cold. Prior to one hearing, I checked the weather report the night before to find that it would be about 30 degrees below zero the next morning when I had to appear in court. The thought of having to place my coat by the bailiff was humiliating, so I left my coat in the car and walked quickly from my car to the building in the freezing cold. Immediately, Randie scolded me, "Where is your coat?" I looked the other way and pretended not to hear her. I answered her later, by cell phone, while sitting in my car after court, with the heat blowing full blast, admitting, "I left my coat in the car because I don't feel as much like a criminal when I have to place it by the bailiff." She was numb. Three years of court hearings and even she hadn't noticed I'd been doing it.

We often felt put down and we always felt oppressed. There was one time when I'd asked the judge not to reappoint CASA. He denied my request, justifying his decision by saying that abiding by his agenda was the trade-off for getting the treatment via the court system. I didn't recall being given any other option. I would be remiss; however, if I didn't acknowledge that of all the court personnel, the judges were the most fair to us. One of them even went out on a limb to get our son into a better treatment center than the choice DCFS had made, and for that, I will be eternally grateful. They usually acknowledged our frequent involvement with our son and never actively encouraged or instigated terminating our parental rights. As the case progressed over the years, I began to detect sadness in the judge's tone regarding our son's lack of therapeutic progress despite the strong support we showed him.

As a foster/adopt parent, I hold a prominent memory at the forefront of my mind. I remember the days of being a foster parent; the days when "permanency" for my son was of paramount importance. This baby, who was found starving to death and had to be fed with an eyedropper once per hour to keep him alive. How all the very same players in the courtroom advocated adamantly for this baby, now my son through adoption, to receive a forever family, and how 13 years later, they are now working to disconnect that tie in the very same courtroom. How quickly the urgency of his "permanency" all went out the window with the $150,000 per year price tag of residential treatment.

Court was always in the morning and I'd go to work after. I generally wear business suits to work because of the nature of our business and the caliber of our clients on Chicago's North Shore. During the first court hearing, a CASA manager kept staring at us. Finally, she came over and introduced herself to me and Jim. She commented that she was staring because she couldn't figure out who those nicely dressed people were. She couldn't figure out if they were attorneys or some other important people. From this we gleaned that most parents didn't wear business attire to court and that parents didn't fall into the category of "important people." I commented privately to Randie about it, who sarcastically answered me with, "It's because you don't have jeans on and you have teeth in your mouth."

Chalk one up for Randie. As much as I hated court, she thrived on it. It was her territory and she owned it. No matter how stressed out I was from the court experience, she could always put me at ease and even make me laugh. She was my saving grace over and over again. How poorly we were treated in court was all such a paradox, considering that simultaneously, I was becoming one of the leading children's mental health advocates in the state.

One week, I'd be in court being treated like a low life and the next I was rubbing elbows with every child mental health advocate in the state, including senatorial and gubernatorial staff. My words were heard and my opinions were respected. I'd risen as a leader amongst the adoptive families and represented them well in important statewide meetings regarding child mental health.

So who am I? A neglectful parent? A leading child advocate? It's all relative based upon which lens you see me through.

Concession

As we approached the permanency hearing ending the close of the third year of our son's second tour as a foster child, I mentioned to my husband that I hadn't been as anxious about court as I'd been in the past. All the other times, I'd been so anxious about court; that I'd needed to take a mild sedative to help me sleep the night before court. I wouldn't need to do that this time and I wasn't really sure why. What was different? I'd been pondering the reason why I wasn't nearly as bothered by it as I'd been in the past. It may have had something to do with a certain federal lawsuit, which I will explain later on. It could have been the fact that I was finally just getting used to it, to an extent that I had never been able to do in the past. My husband had still another thought. He suggested that I'd finally conceded.

In the beginning, we tried to show them what good parents we really were. We had to convince them that we really did love our son and very much wanted what was best for him. Perhaps, I'd finally conceded that they'd never believe us anyway, no matter how we dressed or what we said. I saw myself the way they saw me: a person who had to put her purse and coat by the bailiff and sit in the accused chair; a person who remained silent in that chair while everyone else around her spoke for her child in her place; a person who must remain silent. Silence held while the attorneys and the judge affirmed that yes, we were compliant, yes, we were cooperative, yes, we were making progress towards trying to get our son back. I was a person who sat in the accused chair and made hash marks for each time someone in the court put us down. I had finally internalized the oppression and at least outwardly, accepted it.

Unless there was something to address which negatively affected my son, I just tolerated it. I just didn't have the energy to educate people who didn't care anyway. We'd become victims of systematic oppression.

I conclude that juvenile court is no place for a clinical matter. The court system designed to function for addressing illegal, anti-social, and criminal behavior. They are simply not equipped to manage or process a healthy family who has a child with a complex clinical case.

My mind repeatedly flashed back to a particular court hearing where the judge scolded everyone in the room, except for me and Randie saying, "There is nobody bad here! *Do we all get it?* There is nobody bad here!"

There were no criminals. There was no crime.

Then why were we still here?

"Our lives begin to end the day we become silent about things that matter."

Martin Luther King Jr.

Chapter Eleven

THE CASA DEBACLE

WHILE DANIEL WAS AT THE group home, we received a letter from the CASA organization notifying us that the judge had assigned a CASA volunteer to be Daniel's "voice in court." It said that she'd be scheduling an appointment to meet with us. After the second court hearing, we learned that the CASA volunteer, Judith, had already been to visit our son three times without our knowledge or consent. She had not visited us even once. Apparently, no one had told her that there was no bigger constant in this child's life than his very own parents.

Upon learning this, I called their office to ask why they had sent the letter, but had not yet set up a meeting with us. How could they advocate for our son's "interests" without ever speaking to his parents? A supervisor responded by saying that, as a rule, they never spoke with parents prior to adjudication. That it's just how it is, but since I'd called, she'd make an exception. The supervisor went on to explain in a rather abrupt tone, that they would be our child's constant and that they were not here for us, but for our son.

Judith scheduled an appointment to come to our home to meet us and learn more about the case. She handed me a CASA brochure. She did not consider that we were long time foster parents and were quite familiar with her organization. Unlike the DCFS investigator, she accepted our offer to tour the damage Daniel had done to our house. We'd not had time to fix most of it. She understood that he was aggressive; however she'd been misled about one very important fact. She relayed to us that DCFS told her we didn't *want* our son back. We emphasized to her that quite the opposite was true. We had made decisions which sought out very expensive treatment for our son, while keeping our family safe. As she left, it seemed we were on the same page and we resolved to work together to better the situation for our son and us. Soon after, we suspected she had a different motivation.

Excessive Rule Breaking

Judith was visiting Daniel far too often. We noticed excessive boundary bending and rule violations in the areas of legal, case management, and family.

Judith had a law degree, but to our knowledge, had never formally been employed as an attorney. She advised us to replace our attorney with one that specialized in children's law and that we should log our visits and phone calls to Daniel. This constituted giving legal advice, which she was not allowed to do within the scope of her role as a CASA volunteer. While I was mildly annoyed about this, I chose to overlook it, until she made another mistake at the first school meeting.

I arrived at the new school for Daniel's school placement meeting in the new district. His newly appointed educational surrogate sat next to me in the school lobby. I tried to make small talk with her, as I had also been trained as a DCFS educational surrogate and had served the role for other children. She was polite, but unresponsive. In time, I figured she'd come to understand the situation. I'd just have to be patient.

Many people from the school district entered the small conference room and we joined them. Judith was not present. I was relieved. The caseworker was missing and I wondered why. Daniel came in and sat next to me. He handed me a piece of notebook paper that listed all the reasons he thought he should attend a regular education school, as opposed to a therapeutic or alternative school. Someone was dialed in on teleconference. It was Judith. The therapist's mood lightened and mine soured.

The meeting transpired much better than I'd expected, at least until the final 5 minutes. The therapist at the residential center asked Judith if my husband and I had free access to our son's educational records. I was stunned. Why in the world had he just asked her a question that clearly should have been asked of the caseworker, who was not even there? I was even more flabbergasted at her answer. She answered that we had absolutely *no* access to our son's records before proceeding into a rather lengthy dissertation about how we needed a court order to have access to anything, spoken in a tone which clearly elevated her above me. She was trying to paint us as child abusers to that entire room of school personnel. By the looks of their faces, she succeeded favorably. I was glaring at the therapist. And where *was* the caseworker? I left fuming! I called the caseworker from my car before I ever left the parking lot, to find that she was on vacation. Next, I called her supervisor, who also wondered why he'd not been told about the meeting. When I told him about the meeting's ending conversations, he advised me that he was required to share our son's records with us and that he was thrilled that I attended the meeting because often parents on his caseload don't. He promised to see to it that we were invited to everything and assured me that the caseworker's first responsibility in returning from vacation was to pay a personal visit to the school to straighten it all out. I placed the third call to Randie, who was also now upset at all this unwarranted legal advising.

Judith also decided that Daniel should be in summer school. Acting as Daniel's caseworker, she called the school and directly made arrangements to have him enrolled. CASA volunteers are not trained as caseworkers and are not allowed to function as such. Equally as prohibitive, is participating or interfering with the child's therapy.

Even though reward systems are built into residential programming, Judith interfered with Daniel's therapy by offering him material rewards for reading, never considering that he was already two full grade levels higher than his current grade. Nor did she consider that while he told her he was doing his reading, no one was monitoring her "reward program" and he wasn't even doing it. Thus, it was yet another way for him to get gifts without ever having earned them. And of course, she offered even more rewards for good behavior. Considering all the things he was gaining from her directly, there was no incentive to work hard in therapy, so he didn't.

During our weekly visits to Daniel at the center, he mentioned to us that Judith was buying him gifts. There was something every week. It started out with small gifts at first, but the gifts became increasingly larger and more expensive. However annoying it was to us, it was fairly easy to overlook such things as books, electronic games, and clothing. By the time we got to rollerblades, skateboards, and bicycles, we were raising furrowed eyebrows, and we were beyond upset at the kickboxing lessons, and membership at a national health club chain, complete with personal trainer.

What she didn't know was that he was manipulating her the whole time. Daniel has Obsessive Compulsive Disorder (OCD). He became quite enterprising as he began to buy, sell, and trade the things she'd gotten him to the other residents. He later admitted that he spent hours in his room making lists of things he and the other residents wanted. He'd call her up and ask her to buy him these things. She'd be happy to comply. He'd keep them for himself, or trade for other things he wanted, such as designer shoes. Thus, while we had been working with the therapists to reduce his OCD compulsions, she was simultaneously feeding them. There was yet another way that she was interfering with his therapy.

Judith was sure that Daniel had two problems. He had terrible parents who knew nothing about mental health and he needed far more exercise than we'd provided for him. She intended to solve the latter by providing outdoor exercise equipment and a health club membership. She failed to consider that he already had a family health club membership with us and that spending any more than a nominal amount of money on the child was prohibited.

She took it upon herself to solve the former by taking him out to crowded restaurants so she could teach him how to calm himself down. We alerted her and his therapist that this was not a good idea, in fact, it was downright dangerous. Daniel becomes explosive when he is anxious and this was just the ticket to a public disaster. CASA rules specifically state that the volunteer may never put herself or the child in danger. Purposely creating anxiety for Daniel was double jeopardy considering she was not allowed to participate or instruct in therapeutic practices. When I called to caution her about this, I was blasted with a response that had become her typical retort, "As his CASA, the therapist *and I* will decide what is best for him!"

Stifled by Status

I felt increasingly distressed at all of her infractions. I spoke to the caseworker about it. She responded by saying that the CASA volunteers were overstepping their roles with her as well. She had just confronted another volunteer with major infractions. They needed to choose their battles with the judge and ours would not be one of them. Whenever I brought it up to Randie, she instructed me to remain silent about it. I trusted her judgment. She feared that my complaining about it would reflect poorly to the judge. She didn't want me to appear critical towards anyone in the court system, especially someone the judge appointed. I never felt more oppressed. The situation continued to escalate and finally, Randie, too, drew the line in the sand. Enough was enough. Randie decided it was time to report her to the judge.

When we brought the situation before the judge, DCFS fell silent, supporting neither side. Judith's supervisor and the GAL sided with Judith. We had to attend more court hearings as a result of her overzealousness.

To avoid publicly embarrassing Judith, the judge discussed it with the attorneys in chambers. While they were in chambers, Judith and her supervisor were loudly talking about how I was upset at all the gift giving. They openly discussed giving him even more. The supervisor apologized to Judith for my complaint, continuing that the only person's opinion that counted was hers. "Everyone else," then she outstretched her left arm, palm upwards, and placed her right arm palm down on her left bicep and swept her right arm all the way to the end of the left, culminating in slapping her palms together, in a motion that suggested, "to the moon." The bailiff, the court transcribers, and the DCFS supervisor, who was sitting behind me sat silently. I needed to tell Randie, but I was so addled and humiliated, I was afraid I'd forget what they were saying. I quietly wrote down everything they said. They continued chatting and laughing loudly when the attorneys entered the room. The GAL scowled at them and they stopped.

The judge openly reprimanded Judith for giving legal advice, affirming that is was a major infraction. Then the judge scolded them all, "There is nobody bad here! DO WE ALL GET IT! There is nobody bad here!"

I waited for Randie in the parking lot, who relayed the conversation that transpired in chambers. Wanda was assigned to investigate our complaints. I shared with Randie a synopsis of the CASA behavior within the court room, Randie was flabbergasted. "IN THE COURT ROOM?!" She looked at me in total disbelief. I shared with her the notes I'd taken about the things they'd said when she was in chambers, and demonstrated the supervisor's arm motion as I repeated the story. Randie immediately filed a motion to have Judith dismissed.

Finally, they would see the truth. The judge assigned Wanda to investigate the situation. She would be interviewing everyone, or so we thought.

Biased Investigation

Wanda interviewed Judith, who downplayed her actions and omitted a lot of details. She interviewed Daniel, who lied because he didn't want the flow of gifts to stop. She interviewed the therapists, who had no clue what the CASA volunteer role even was, and said they thought she was therapeutic. We waited for our turn to be interviewed, *which never came.* We were oppressed once again. We were never interviewed at all. I thought we were doomed. I considered giving up. How could we get this moving in the right direction when the court personnel were pushing us deeper and deeper into systematic oppression? We felt that we had no voice in court whatsoever. The odds were all stacked against us. I feared we were about to lose our son forever.

Judith explained her behavior by minimizing the amount and value of the gifts. She assured them that she added him to her health club membership at no charge and that the personal training was free. I don't know if anyone ever verified this with the health club, nonetheless, it was preposterous to think that anyone could be added to a major health club at no charge. Personal trainers charge top wages in their field; it was obvious that was not free. Ultimately, no one believed her.

Jim was working out of state at the time. I had to face all of this alone. The night before the court date to address Judith's behavior, I didn't sleep. I feared they failed to see the truth and were all against me. I was a nervous wreck. However, when I entered the court room, surprisingly, an unexpected sense of calm and courage swept over me. I walked through the metal detector and glanced towards the CASA office. Judith was not milling around as usual. She was sitting in a chair outside the court room with her head down. A man was sitting next to her holding her hand. He scowled at me. I wondered who he was. Then it occurred to me, it must be her husband. What was he doing here? CASA volunteers had to sign a confidentiality agreement agreeing not to discuss the case with anyone except other CASA volunteers. They couldn't even discuss it with their spouse. It was yet another infraction. Judith's supervisor appeared and sat next to her, consoling her, never asking her husband to leave. Her husband remained in the lobby when the case was called. Two CASA managers entered the courtroom along with Judith.

Turning Point

The judge noted that this CASA volunteer was a distraction, thanking her for her service before dismissing her. The judge requested a replacement. Randie requested that the judge not appoint another CASA volunteer. The judge denied the request, noting that there were some things we'd have to accept as long as our son remained a ward of the state.

It was over. She was gone. Judith's manager consoled her as they exited the courtroom. The other CASA manager shot me a stern look of disgust as I passed by her on my way out of the courtroom. I paused for a second, made firm eye contact with her, and fired the same facial expression right back.

Somehow we'd prevailed without anyone even allowing us to reveal all that had really happened. I reveal the details of that ordeal in this writing for the very first time.

Betrayal Exposed

With a sigh of relief, I visited Daniel and told him what happened. We suspected that she was trying to get the no-fault dependency case amended to abuse. I'll never forget the look on Daniel's face, which spoke of complete betrayal. He came forth with even more infringements. He was calling her house every week asking her to buy him things. Some of the gifts she bought were over one hundred dollars. He was speaking to her on the telephone more than to us. Once, he even spoke to her husband, at length, on the phone. So that's why Judith's husband was sitting in the court lobby that day. I told Daniel her husband was there; perhaps ready to testify against me. Daniel also disclosed that Judith had been badmouthing Wanda to him, criticizing her legal skills. I assured him that Wanda had been around a long time, and I had confidence in her abilities, even though she had supported Judith rather than me. Daniel admitted he used Judith for material gain. He hugged me and told me he felt badly for almost trading away his family for material things he wanted. While we saw right through her from the very beginning, her escapades had duped him completely. I shared with him that it was really Randie's efforts that truly saved him from losing the most important people in his life. He was mad at himself for not catching on. He hugged me and apologized for putting me through it all. That day, he learned who truly cared about him. Daniel promised that he would never again take someone else's word over his father's and mine.

I also asked him to come clean with Wanda and confess that he lied to her about how extensive the gift giving was. He was so embarrassed; he couldn't do it. About a year later, he carried the guilt over it long enough. He finally confessed to her that he lied about it and apologized for his actions. This was such a huge step of progress for him and I was so proud of him for having done it. Sadly, Wanda replied, "It's okay. If I were you, I would have lied too." When he told me that, I felt a tinge of betrayal once again. It was a missed opportunity for an important adult in his life to teach him about the importance of honesty and that adults fall prey to temptation sometimes too. Instead, she made light of his mistake.

More than a Number

Month after month, we waited for "the call" notifying us of the new CASA volunteer. It came in five months' time, and this time, it was a man. We surmised the switch in gender was by design. Brody left a message on my answering machine. He said he was calling about number #08CJ01.* Was he referring to Daniel? Was my son #08CJ01? I sprinted to the file cabinet and grabbed one of the court documents. I spied the same number in the upper right hand corner, identified as the case number. He referred to Daniel, not by his name, but by a number. I was reeling for a minute. At first, I was extremely hurt. How could anyone refer to my son, that I love so much, as a number? As I processed the pain, I considered the possibility that if he viewed my son as nothing more than a number, perhaps, he wouldn't be so over-involved. I dreaded having to meet with him. I reluctantly set up an appointment with him.

Mistrust Deepens

He arrived with another man. They made an excuse about needing to ride together because of poor road conditions, due to the weather. It was winter, but the roads were clear. It was a lie. They asked permission for both of them to come in. We felt we had to say yes. We did not want to appear uncooperative. They offered an empty apology. They were very sorry about "whatever happened," eluding that the prior debacle was an embarrassment to their organization. They tried to appease us by repeating what the judge had said, that there was nobody bad here.

Both men appeared at the DCFS Administrative Case Review, the following week. They stated that the other man was a CASA supervisor and asked permission for him to sit in on the meeting. Again, we felt we had no choice but to allow it. We did not want to appear uncooperative. We later found out that they lied to us about the other man's position. The man claiming to be a supervisor, in fact, was not. We discovered he was sworn into the organization just months before Brody. Years of being friends with Randie, who was a criminal attorney by profession, had taught me well. I had heard her repeat a certain phrase so often; I could recite it in my sleep. *"Don't lie about anything that can be verified."*

We suspect that the two men came together because they were trying to mask the fact that it was Brody's first case. We surmised that they were concerned that we'd uncover the fact that Brody was, in fact, a rookie, fresh out of CASA training. The organization sought to regain our confidence in them. His superiors were wary that his non-experience would fail to regain the trust they badly sought to recover. They knew that we were highly upset about their prior representative's escapades and feared sending Brody into the "lion's den."

Despite their efforts, any attempts at redeeming themselves were gone. We simply didn't trust them. Neither did Daniel.

Brody attempted to walk the fence between getting his court reports done and not rubbing us the wrong way. Daniel didn't trust him enough to tell him anything. At one point, Brody insisted that he "observe" a visit at our home between us and Daniel. We felt completely humiliated. How quickly he forgot "there is nobody bad here." We were once again being evaluated under the "abuse lens." It was total degradation. We inquired as to his reasoning. This was not an abuse or neglect case. DCFS did not require supervised visits. He replied, "The court gives me the ability to observe Daniel in any setting I choose. I will watch you visit your son, *because I can*." If we refused his request, he threatened to report badly to the court about us. Denigration. Oppression. We were in our 50's. We had successfully raised three other children. We were long time foster-adopt parents and the court was continuing to dehumanize us, insisting that we be babysat by a total stranger who knew nothing about us or our son. Brody was unconcerned about our feelings about it. He had a volunteer job to do.

Before the visit could take place, Daniel's behavior escalated severely, causing him to miss many days of school attendance. He was damaging property at the school and at the center. Emotionally, he was falling apart. We begged the therapist to call off the dogs. Daniel didn't need caseworkers and CASA's. He just needed his mom and dad. The therapist asked Brody to delay visiting until Daniel stabilized.

Shortly thereafter, the residential center announced it would be closing its doors. Daniel would have to be placed elsewhere. DCFS attempted to put Daniel in a center that specialized in juvenile delinquents. We fought against them for three months to get him into the only center in the state that understood trauma issues. It was 5 ½ hours from our home. There was talk about reassigning a new CASA volunteer local to the area where Daniel would be living. Brody and his associates recused themselves from the case due to the distance. We never had to endure that humiliating "observation" through CASA's "abuse lens." For that I am very, very grateful.

Familiar Eyes and Ears—the Parents

We asked the judge to proceed without them. This time, she allowed it, reminding us that she could change her mind at any time. It was her call. We finally succeeded in removing one wedge between Daniel and us, but it took us two years to accomplish it.

The Role of CASA

This has long been the one arm of the case that I find it the most difficult to be objective. Given our family's bad experience with them, it would be easy enough to kick them to the curb; however, I'm sure there are countless children whom the organization has actually helped. Despite my personal battle scars, suffice it to say that in the grand scheme of things, they do more good than harm. At the same time, I will stand on one issue regarding the CASA organization. They have 40 hours of training in neglect and abuse cases. They have *zero* hours in no-fault dependency and psychiatric lockout cases. CASA should be appointed to the cases in which they were trained for, which include abuse, neglect, and dependency cases in which the child has no parent to guide him. If the governments would commit to providing mental healthcare for the state's most critically ill children, no-fault dependency cases would not even exist. The "eyes and ears" of the court should continue to be the same people who have always been them, the child's parents. Some judges refuse to recognize this, because they get stuck into doing things the usual way rather than treating the case on its own merits.

As a two decade foster-adopt parent, I have seen a vast difference in the operation of CASA in the same time frame. Long ago, we never noticed them. They mysteriously appeared at a meeting, sat unobtrusively in the back of the room, took their notes, and disappeared just as quickly. I read an article wherein the volunteers complained about having too many limitations and not being able to do enough for the kids. In my opinion, they have strayed too far from the original purposes and intents of their role, which was to be objective fact takers and passive observers. They no longer sit at the back of the room, rather taking center stage, over-stepping the attorneys, caseworkers, therapists, foster parents, and certainly the parents. It was never a role that was intended to create a strong personal bond with the child, which causes loss of objectivity. That kind of relationship is reserved for the people who love and care for the child on a daily basis or who otherwise have family ties with the child. CASA has crossed over from objective to subjective and from passive to active, defeating the original purpose of their role. CASA volunteers can make a difference in the life of a child, but they must do so within the boundaries of their positions. If volunteers truly desire to have a stronger relationship with children, I suggest that they trade in their 10 hour per month CASA lanyard for a 24/7 foster care license. If they truly want to make a difference, they can begin with the mentally ill teens living in residential centers that have no families to call or visit them.

Our experience with CASA is just one of many examples of how quickly things can go awry when a clinical case is mismanaged as a child welfare case. Any professional along the way can misperceive the case, shifting it towards a detrimental course. In our case, the culprit was CASA. In speaking with other families with a psychiatric lockout case, the culprit was a caseworker, a judge, or an attorney.

As in the case of one family, the GAL and states attorney concurred that if the single mom from the south side of Chicago couldn't afford the $150,000 per year of mental health care, her son didn't deserve to have his adoption preserved. This mother was charged with abuse and neglect in juvenile court. Her attorney was able to stop the state's attorney and GAL from terminating her parental rights. If the attorney had been unsuccessful, her son would have been lost in the foster care system forever. Apparently, no one had told the state's attorney that foster parents weren't exactly clamoring for the 11 year old boy with bipolar disorder and schizophrenia, or that he already had a mother who loved him. (Identical to our son, her son's medical needs were covered under the EPSDT provision of federal Medicaid law all along, and she should never have lost guardianship. This provision is discussed in Chapter 16.)

In another case, it was a judge, who refused to amend the neglect charge to no-fault dependency, which caused the parents' names to remain on the

State Central Register of indicated perpetrators for five years, solely because they had a mentally ill child; who was refused treatment.

In still another case, it was the caseworker who showed reverse racial prejudice. The parents were Caucasian and the adoptive children were African American. She, along with her supervisor, who was also African American, saw an investigation as a means for taking custody of the family's other children, attempting to return them to the African American community. This caused the family's younger children to be removed from the only home they had ever known for 6 months, emotionally traumatizing them and their parents, unnecessarily.

There is inherent risk in processing clinical cases as abuse cases. Any professional involved can get it wrong, anywhere along the way, and sever family ties unnecessarily.

I sometimes wonder if my heart will ever heal from the emotional damage CASA did to my son and to me. Whenever I recall this period of time, the very same word haunts me every time.

Betrayal.

*The case number was changed to protect confidentiality.

"Just because you reach a certain age, does not mean you are miraculously cured of all the things you've endured."

Katie Beckett

Chapter Twelve

EMOTIONAL DAMAGE TO THE CHILD

THE CHILD ALSO SUFFERS mentally, emotionally, and therapeutically while the parents are being criminalized in exchange for treatment. The system, by virtue of child welfare and court personnel acting in loco parentis, or in lieu of parents, works directly counterproductive to trauma therapy. As the systematic wedge drives into the child's life, the child moves from perpetrator to victim and from patient to plaintiff. Ironically, this all happens under the smoke screen of "family reunification."

Fears

The immediate emotion for the child is fear. Children with mental and/or emotional illness often have severe anxiety disorders. They may suffer from organic psychological phobias. The child may experience fear of the unknown, fear of interrogation, confusion, fear of separation and loss of family, loss of identity, and unresolved grief and abandonment. These fears infiltrate the child's soul, exacerbating his already compromised emotional state.

Why fear? Because the child welfare investigators approach the situation with a neglect-abuse lens. They go through the normal investigative process, undeterred by the fact that it was caused by an unpreventable psychiatric lockout. They interrogate the child, questioning him over and over whether his parents abused him. "Did they hit you, did they yell at you, did they spank you, did they give you food, did you have access to the toilet, did you have fresh drinking water, did you ever have broken bones, or bruises from your parents..."

Even once the initial investigation is over, the caseworker interrogates him at least monthly. If CASA is assigned, he will also interrogate the child monthly. Though he just approaches it in a friendlier sort of way, it is an interrogation nonetheless. The GAL also has a standard litany of questions he or she asks, generally in the weeks before court hearings. There are others including monitors, case reviewers, educational liaisons, and educational surrogates. If there were a funding source for treatment available, none of these people would even be involved. While these workers take pride in their jobs for efficiently filling out their forms, the child starts to resent the seemingly endless stream of strangers encroaching upon the spot being held within his family.

The child feels increasing separation from his family and non-verbal threat of abandonment, causing fear that he will lose his family forever. He suffers feelings of loss, abandonment, and grief. But the "system" with all its "help" does not offer any support for the child's feelings. For adoptive children, this is double jeopardy. They have already experienced these feelings over losing their birth families. This stirs the pot, conjuring up even more feelings of worthlessness and grief over loss of family for the second time (many times for some). When children lose a parent to death, they may attend grief therapy, however, when a child loses a family to the system, they do not. In psychiatric lockout cases, grief and grief counseling are preventable consequences.

Separation from family is difficult for children, even for short periods. They regularly miss family birthdays, graduations, weddings, anniversaries, holidays, and other special family events. Initially, we sent our son to a residential center believing he'd be treated and return home within a year.

Our four children are five years apart. Daniel was 13 years old when he left for residential care, so our oldest child was 18 years old at the time. He expected time to stand still while he was away. He was certain that he'd return home a better son and brother and when he did, we could pick up where we all left off. He never fathomed that his siblings would grow up without him. In the three years he's lived in a residential setting, we've had 3 high school graduations, one college graduation (mine, thank you), one military boot camp graduation, one wedding, and a host of birthdays, anniversaries, holidays, and other celebrations. He's missed almost all of them and we've missed having him in attendance. As I posed for family photos at my oldest son's wedding, I couldn't help but feel misty that our youngest son was not in the photo with us. That day, I stifled the tears for Mason and Katy's sake. It was their day and I didn't want to spoil it by being emotional over something I had no control over.

He worried about his future almost as much as we did. Would he ever be able to go to school and not become violent? Would he ever be able to obtain a college degree or hold down a job? If he couldn't have healthy relationships with his family, how could he ever be married or have children? Would he someday end up homeless or in jail? These are common fears and questions amongst people dealing with mental illness, but Daniel's emotional pain was exacerbated by a system that sought to drive away his strongest support system, his family. Sadly, the family he feared losing, did not want to lose him either. When the state legally slated him in direct opposition to us, it hurt the entire family.

Caseworkers tell the child his parents are "in trouble," followed by months of no family contact in person or even by phone. The child is told nothing, not when he can speak with his parents, if ever. Simply, "Your parents are in trouble with the law." Anxiety for the child increases as the child suspects his parents are being criminalized in exchange for his treatment, elevating the anxiety to an all-time high and causing his condition to worsen.

Methodically, during one of her visits, the caseworker hands the child a nice little handbook, called "Putting the Pieces Together." Pamphlet #330 is a DCFS pamphlet designed to help the child understand the complex child welfare system and the barrage of intrusive adults that have now infiltrated his life. In reading its 32 pages, the child will read 19 times that his parents will be given time to make positive changes in their lives, in order that he may return home. The pamphlet also outlines what options exist, if his parents, for whatever reason, do not make positive changes in their lives. Good intentions aside, it sends a clear message to a child that his parents are bad people who are in trouble, and that his illness is completely their fault.

Meanwhile the parents take the fall for the child's mental illness; numerous other "helpers" are systematically driving a wedge between the parent and child.

Systematic Wedge

The system drives a professional wedge between the child and his family. Investigators have sold an "abusive parent" policy to the child. Caseworkers, already overloaded with neglect and abuse cases, replace parents as guardians. The GAL establishes attorney-client privilege. CASA presents the child's perspective to the court. The educational surrogate stands as his guardian in educational matters. With so many bases filled, parents retreat to the bench. There is no room for the parent to represent the child, and even when they desire to do so, the others won't allow it.

Case Management

The child is continually interrogated about his relationship with his family, though child welfare is the organization that drove them away in the first place. This is confusing to a child (and to the family). Drive the family away, heal the child, then reunite the family, but do it all under the guise of "family reunification." Our case was once referred to by a DCFS caseworker as a "disrupted adoption." The child welfare and juvenile justice systems fail to recognize that we did not "disrupt" it. They did. The child feels emotional pain and separation as he watches his parents be systematically oppressed, and catapulted out to left field.

The child must now call his caseworker if he needs clothing, a haircut, or wants to see his family. I specifically recall three specific examples regarding how we were overshadowed by others.

One day, my son expressed his frustration to me that he didn't want to have to call a caseworker so he could go on a school field trip, elaborating; that they take too long to call back. He told me sadly, "I just wanted to call my mom."

After fighting against DCFS in court for three months to get Daniel admitted to the only trauma treatment center in Illinois, we asked and received permission to drive him to the new placement. We were greeted with a warm and friendly reception. "Welcome Daniel" signs were posted in several places. They fed us a nice lunch and gave us a tour of the campus. We met the various staff members who'd be working with our son. They even presented him with a pillowcase that had our family photos ironed onto it, to help him feel closer to us during his treatment there. They assured us that they'd be working with all of us towards the goal of safely bringing him home. We were all feeling pretty good about our decision to place him there, until it was time for the paperwork.

When it was time to complete the admissions packet, we filled in their blanks and answered their questions. It was a stark contrast from his entry to the first residential treatment center, where he'd been deposited from the group home by a total stranger, after being programmed that his parents were criminals. This time, it was different. This time, we admitted him as a family unit based upon a family decision. When we finished the first set of papers, our son's mood soured. He hung his head and stated that he hated seeing the letters DCFS stamped on the guardian line. He pouted and turned away. He stood up from the table and went to sit on the couch behind the small conference table. He asked us to finish the rest without him. In a state of numbness, out of my peripheral vision; I detected a small tear trickling from the corner of my husband's eye. Mine shortly followed, as if his vulnerability gave me permission to weep quietly as well. The reality set in for all three of us. The staff offered us tissues. They'd witnessed this before.

While we were deeply hurt by those incidents along with many others, the most disturbing memory is sitting in a clinical staffing, where the caseworker told Daniel directly, "You must listen to *me* because you are *my* child." Startling everyone in the room, Daniel shouted back at her, "I'm NOT your child, I BELONG TO MY PARENTS!" She frowned and snapped back, "Whatever!" That incident remains a deep wound for all three of us.

GAL

The GAL is hired by the state to provide legal representation for the child in court. With so little financial resources for mental health to go around, we often wondered why the government was so willing to dole out money to the juvenile court system to process cases which had no legal bearing. The ways in which a GAL drives a wedge between parent and child include: failing to factor the parent/child relationship, standing in opposition to the parents, allowing kids to manipulate the system for personal gain, and threatening to sever family ties. Once again, these are all major bonding and attachment issues for post-adoptive children. The therapists seek to strengthen bonds, while the court weakens them.

While some children feel guilty that parents are being punished in exchange for their treatment, defending their parents to the court personnel, others, less mentally and emotionally strong, may fall victim to taking a stand against their parents. This may be due to the nature of the mental/emotional condition, or due to systematic mental erosion. The child thinks, "If the system constantly treats my parents as 'bad' people, perhaps they are." The child then turns against his parents. The fact that the child/family relationship was already stressed due to mental instability and multiple hospitalizations, this new revelation by the child, expedites the erosion. If the therapists don't take an active and early stance towards family restoration and against systematic oppression, and often they don't, the family unit is doomed, and the child's strongest level of support leaves with it.

On our case, we were never really quite sure where we stood with any of the GAL's. At first they responded to it as no-fault dependency, speaking highly of our efforts and parenting skills to the judge. When CASA tried to sway the court against us, the tables clearly turned against us. When we fought against DCFS to get Daniel into an appropriate treatment center, the GAL swayed to our side once again. In the final days, she shunned us. While we have long demonstrated that we are the people closest to our son and have always held his bests interests dear to our hearts, never along the way, did the GAL ever interview us regarding his needs or care. Of course, we did stand in opposition to her in court and witnessed her referring to our son as "my client." We knew that she had the power to concur with others in terminating our parental rights if she so chose.

Perhaps the ultimate tragedy is if the court personnel are successful in turning the child against his family and the judge actually does follow through on termination of parental rights. While this has not happened to us, the CASA debacle certainly brought us close, and other families have been threatened as well. Even if complete termination does not happen, the threat consistently and morbidly looms over the child and family like a dark cloud.

CASA

I list CASA as another entity that drives a wedge between child and parent. It is one more person who attempts to fill the parent's shoes. I toyed around with which chapter to include our tragic epics with them and finally decided it merited a chapter of its own, thus the brevity of this section. I will only add that overstepping the parent role increases the emotional toll to the child and family incrementally. They simply can't afford to get it wrong.

Educational Surrogate

For whatever reason, educational surrogates never seemed to last. I surmise they quit for the same reason I did when I was one. They really don't do much other than show up and sign the papers. It's hardly worth anyone's time. Nonetheless, seeing yet another stranger's name on the paper was disturbing to Daniel and to us.

When getting notice of an IEP or other meeting, it was addressed to Daniel and Daniel's guardian, i.e. educational surrogate "name of the quarter." The list of attendees was listed in the body of the letter with Daniel's parents slated dead last. Sometimes they left us out completely and we got the notice after the meeting was held. We always called to remind them that we'd been forgotten once again. It was disappointing to Daniel not to have his parents attend his school functions and to have yet another stranger signing on his parents' dotted line.

Stigma

I often refer to my son's diagnoses as "the alphabet soup." ADHD, OCD, PTSD..." In addition to being awarded all the alphabet soup labels, according to proper diagnoses, the system labels him with a few more, stigmatizing him further: DCFS child, state ward, CASA child. The child wishes to be void of all labels, preferring to simply be referred to by his name.

If the effects of child emotional pain and family separation are not enough, the child is further victimized by therapeutic setbacks.

Systematic Hindrance to Bonding and Attachment Therapy

Systematic backlog causes treatment delays and children's cases are queued up on lists for staffings. During this time, the child's treatment is put on hold. Without treatment, the child sees an open door to manipulate caregivers and others, which causes additional therapeutic setback.

Because of interview and paper intensive procedures, the child sits in limbo during various stages of the case management process. During this time, the child finds ways to use whoever is easy and convenient, to get what he wants. There is a gang-like culture amongst kids in group homes and residential centers where they learn from each other how to survive and get around the system. Survival mode takes precedence over moving forward in therapy while negative habits take root, including lying, stealing, and scheming.

The lag also causes a child to lose valuable treatment time. The child treatment team changes, causing therapeutic delays while new relationships form and trust builds. Trust is a major issue in therapy. As each adult fails the child, he loses, rather than gains trust, bouncing him backwards, rather than moving him forward. Court personnel are not trained in mental health issues. As a result, they can do more harm than good. Traumatized children feel the need to be in constant control and while the therapists try to regulate this urge, the child is manipulating the court personnel for personal gain. The court personnel are ignorant to how the child is "playing them" and don't have time to gain scope of the situation, so manipulation continues and therapeutic progress is stampeded.

It is natural and expected for all adoptive children to address adoptive issues at some point in their lives. Some adoptive families prefer to keep adoptions closed, while others find it beneficial to have an open adoption. At some point, most adoptees come to terms with abandonment issues. They question who gave them up and why, desiring to know the circumstances which led to the adoption. For many kids, these feelings drudge up thoughts and feelings of abandonment which have to be addressed by the adoptive parents or in therapy. For the second time foster child, this is doubly distressing. The child has already at least once had to address his own issues of security and abandonment and is once again, having to do it all over again, in relation to his second family. He experiences grief over the loss, which includes:

- Shock and denial
- Pain and guilt
- Anger and bargaining
- Depression, reflection and loneliness

The Systemic Wedge

During the process of re-addressing adoption issues, he also has to address the trauma issues that victimized him during his first tour as a foster child, and now has a second set of trauma issues to be addressed in therapy due to the second tour as foster child.

Many children who were traumatized as infants, toddlers, or small children, can be healed from their trauma using bonding and attachment based therapies, such as those suggested by Dr. Ronald Federici, Dr. Bruce Perry, and Dr. Daniel Hughes. Trauma therapy is based upon increasing the emotional bond between the child and parent and helping the child build a stronger attachment to his parents. The stronger the bond, the easier it is for the child to let go of his need to provide for himself. When he is able to let go and allow his parents to care for him and nurture him, he feels secure enough in his strongest relationships, allowing him to let go of his need to be in control of himself. He lets others into his heart and trusts them to provide for his basic needs which include food, shelter, affection, love, nurturing, and attention. As bonding and attachment with his parents strengthens; his security level increases incrementally. Simultaneously, his anxiety decreases allowing him the ability to better regulate his emotions and attain true emotional healing.

With a basic understanding of bonding and attachment therapies, it is easy to see how the child needs to see his parents in the foreground and other adults in the background. By forcing the pre-adoptive traumatized child back into the foster care system to access treatment, and allowing strangers to sub for his parents, custody relinquishment works in direct opposition to the bonding and attachment therapies for which the treatment team is working so hard to achieve. Instead of moving the child forward in therapy and closer to returning home, he is actually moving further away from both goals.

"The Systemic Wedge"
Educational Surrogate
States Attorney
Caseworker
Child CASA Parent
Judge
GAL

When a child must live in a residential placement for the safety of himself and others, we cannot completely erase the increased sense of fear and trauma. However, by admitting him with the full love and support of his family, it can be reduced drastically. What can and should be avoided, especially for post-adoptive children is the legal separation from the very people he was supposed to have been bonding with since his adoption. The barrage of legal "helpers" increase the problems caused by the initial trauma, all of which stem from his lack of ability to bond and attach to his parents.

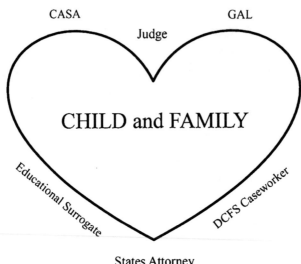

Family Preservation

CASA   GAL

Judge

CHILD and FAMILY

Educational Surrogate   DCFS Caseworker

States Attorney

DCFS contracts with therapeutic providers, who are training post adoptive parents in the areas of trauma and attachment. However, once it becomes evident that the child needs a residential placement, the same folks steer the family away from residential treatment centers which actively implement bonding and attachment therapies such as play therapy and other trust-based programs.

While the parents feel pressure over the race against time to heal the child before adulthood, the entire system is fighting the process.

Not everything made you stronger. It was possible to survive, yet still be crippled for your trouble. Sometimes it was okay to run away, to skip the test, to chicken out. Or at least to get some help."

Scott Westerfield

Chapter Thirteen

EMOTIONAL DAMAGE TO THE FAMILY UNIT

Coming to Terms with Relinquishment

ADVOCATE, DIXIE JORDAN GIVES the introduction to Karl Dennis' and Dr. Ira Lourie's book, "Everything is Normal Until Proven Otherwise." In giving scope to her own feelings of how she was perceived as a parent of a child with multiple mental health diagnoses she says,

"What I remember is the unspoken accusation and implied responsibility that came with the diagnoses and that hung, almost visibly, in the air before settling across my shoulders like a mantle of lead."

That sentiment struck a strong chord with me the day that I read it. One day when I was feeling particularly frustrated and oppressed, the caseworker tried to allay my fears by telling me that no one was judging me. This was not a true statement. We have been judged from the beginning. When a child has cancer, it's Mother Nature's fault, it's God's fault, it's genetics' fault. When a child has mental health issues, it's generally perceived as the parent's fault. Maybe it was never verbalized, but it was always there. Sometimes it *was* verbalized, like a lone report in our child neglect investigation that stuck out like a sore thumb from all the positive ones.

It was hard enough to attend family gatherings and other functions with our son, who never seemed to be able to hold it together. We kept much of the seriousness of our son's illness hidden from our families. We truly believed Daniel would improve with all the wraparound services we put into place for him. Because our families didn't know what we were really dealing with, it was difficult for them to understand why we kept him in such close proximity to one of us at family gatherings or why we often arrived late and left early. It was even harder when people outside of our families lay blame for the symptoms of post-traumatic stress disorder, on our parenting ability.

It is an easy thing for some people to say that they would never, never succumb to a psychiatric lockout. Drawing on the recollection of the four choices that we had when we came to the psychiatric lockout crossroads, we have played those conversations over and over again in our minds in an attempt to discover if there was really any other way to deal with the lose-lose situation that we were facing. Every time, we came up with the same answer. No, there was nothing else that we could have or would have done differently. However, it still hasn't relieved us of the guilt that we felt in having done it.

Yet, whenever there is a news story about a family who found themselves out of their league in caring for a mentally ill child and was forced to relinquish him back to the state after being refused treatment, every news reporter colored the story the same way.

"The parents want to give him back."

I spoke directly with a fair number of those parents and they all said the same thing. They didn't wish to give their child back. What they really wanted was the same thing that we wanted. They wanted treatment and family preservation. They just couldn't figure out how to keep everyone safe while caring for their child at home. And every time it happened, people wanted to know how I felt about it. The internet counters on the short video about our son and my personal blog skyrocketed. People knew I'd be writing about it and sought my opinion.

Even though I was becoming an expert on such topics as trauma related diagnoses, system of care issues, and EPSDT, there were still those, in the general public, who insinuated that what we did was wrong. The contrast was made clear during a conversation between me and Randie, who has clearly been on our side every step of the way, when I snapped at her,

"They took my son because he is sick!"

She retorted, "You locked him out!"

Well, there it was. Both sides in black and white.

Randie's perspective was split and I came to understand that she had her own reasons for taking one side or the other. As a mother, and someone who loved my son almost as much as I did, she often sympathized with my perspective. She successfully portrayed us to the court as responsible and cooperative parents. She groomed us as to how to present an acceptable image, thus protecting our interests regarding our son. As an attorney, who in her peer's eyes needed to be seen as the professional that kept her client walking the straight and narrow, she sometimes took their viewpoint. Her focus usually weighed heavier on her role within the court, rather than succumbing to our feelings of denigration and oppression. The courtroom was her place of business and would continue to be so for many more years, whereas our plight would eventually end. She walked the fence between attorney and friend better than anyone else could have done.

On still another day, she and I met odds when another attorney was encouraging us to go public with our story. She feared that her connections in the juvenile court would see it as treason and it would reflect badly upon us and also upon her career.

I told the other attorney, that from day one, we decided we would stand on the truth. No matter what happened, we were solid and we intended to stand on it. We had no control over where the chips fell. We had no control over who thought or said anything, but we were completely responsible for everything we said and stood for. I hadn't said anything in any public or private arena that I could not or would not back up with truth and solid fact.

What we stood on was that we hadn't failed our son. We'd rallied around him stronger and longer than most parents ever could.

We weren't the ones to blame for what happened. It was the government's fault. It failed us. Worse, it failed our son.

Grief

The one thing that none of us was prepared for was experiencing the pain of separation and grief. It felt like death! Our son was gone, but we were hanging onto a part of him. Sometimes it was only by a thread, but we always hung tightly to that thread.

Like our son, we also experienced grief through our ordeal. We experienced every stage of it. And there were other times when grief snuck up on us when we weren't expecting it, like walking down the hall, past his bedroom, peeking in even though we knew it was empty. And doing it over and over again, still knowing it was empty, wondering when he'd be able to sleep in there again. Certain milestones that we celebrated every year went by. His annual piano recital and piano guild, Irish dance competitions and performances. We watched his peers growing up and going through all the awful, normal teen years. We had stopped attending many events that we'd gone to in the past. Now, there was no reason to go.

Following the somber stages, grief moves to the healing stages which include:

- Upward Turn
- Reconstruction
- Acceptance and Hope

These are the stages that enable you to heal and move forward. When you lose a part of your child to the state for mental health reasons, you never progress to the healing stages. There is no healing. There is no sense of closure. You just repeatedly cycle through the first stages of grief.

Prior to being forced to trade custody rights for mental healthcare, we felt trapped. We had no answers and nowhere to turn for help. After the lockout, we still felt trapped. The system had caught us in its net and we couldn't find our way out. We tried to repair the system of care net so that we could navigate our way out, and that didn't work either. No matter what choices we made, there were no appropriate options, which brought us to the place where our son received treatment, and the rest of us remained safe. We lived in a state of constant fear.

Fear

In taking this drastic step of trading custody rights for treatment, we continued to face some old fears as well as added new fears to the list. We lost some of our ability to exercise normal parent decision-making. We had long feared that we might never figure out how to stabilize his condition. We became increasingly concerned about the prospects for his future. More worrisome than all of that was that we might lose our parental rights all together.

For so long, we couldn't get anyone to help us get decisions made for his treatment and suddenly, they were being made right and left without our consent or knowledge. We were torn about whether it was better to have limited choices that were not appropriate or no choices at all. DCFS was selecting the facilities with minimal input from us. They dictated what meetings we had to appear at and when, and there were an abundance of them. They also dictated who else attended the meetings and what input they were allowed to give or what we were allowed to sign, which was usually not much. DCFS, CASA, and the GAL were all interviewing our son on a regular basis behind our backs. We couldn't even sign for so much as an aspirin for him. DCFS controlled how much money he got and how he spent it. We wondered if they would ever polish off the rest of the parental rights we'd managed to salvage. And some of the old fears have never left us either.

We'd never gotten Daniel stable. The closest we'd come was when I didn't work and he was home with me full time. For that period of time, we'd managed to keep him out of the hospital, but staying on top of his moods and behavior was a full time job. The longer he was unstable we became confused as to what stability would look like for him. We didn't and still don't know what qualifies as normal for him. Because he has never gone any length of time and kept stable, we have continued to worry about his future and what it holds. We had our son to deal with, we had the system to deal with, and we were still trying to hold our heads above water dealing with the rest of the family and normal everyday life.

Systematic Oppression

In dealing with our ordeal as long as we have, for better or worse, it has really brought each one of our family members right down to the very core of who we really are. It has brought out the very best and the very worst in each and every one of us. At the same time we never really changed the fiber of who we were at the root. Sometimes, and usually temporarily, we molded to fit into the box that others needed to see us in, so that we could retain the rest of our parental rights. I say temporarily, because no one was able to keep *me* cooped up for long. Through everything, and to everyone, I was the hero or the villain.

Chapter 18 speaks to my perspective on how our nation came to accept the barbaric concept of custody relinquishment. All along, within my own mind, I kept comparing our situation to other groups who'd been severely oppressed: the Jews, the slaves.

Within child welfare, it didn't matter what kind of job we had or how nice of a house we lived in. It didn't matter that our other three kids were all community servants or that we'd put together the biggest wraparound program for our son anyone had ever seen. No matter how hard we worked to stay involved or how much we did, they made us feel like we were never quite good enough and never quite deserving enough. For those who too eagerly and earnestly took over our parenting roles, we were never anything more than the "stinkin' parents."

We were always being replaced by someone and often we were not invited to things at all. I had homeschooled all four of my children for 8 years and had served as an educational surrogate for other DCFS wards; yet they always wanted to appoint an educational stand-in for our son. I had a pang of angst every time she signed in my place. Apparently, I was up to snuff for other kids, just not for my own son.

We were robbed of some of our most basic fundamental civil rights. We didn't always know where our son was or how he was. Sometimes we had to have permission to visit him or to bring him home. We didn't have as much opportunity to spend with him in teaching, training, and guiding him through his adolescent years. We were constantly being coerced, threatened, interrogated and spied upon. We were spoken to as if we were neglectful or abusive or spoken about as if we were not present at all. We often felt as though we got shoved to the children's table at Thanksgiving dinner. As time went on, while our visits were not directly supervised, the caseworker might be "observing" and evaluating us from a distance. As much as our son expressed his displeasure at being referred to as "our child" by total strangers; we disliked hearing it just as much. And we hated that it hurt him. We often felt demoralized and defeated.

After the first year, Jim and I had an emotional shift. Jim worked in another state for the first year of our ordeal, so the bulk of the meetings and court dates fell to me. I was stressed and bitter. When the economy sank and the building trades faltered, Jim returned home and took over most of the meetings and court dates to give me a break from it. He relayed the most recent events to me one day. He was angry and bitter. He sounded like me. Whichever of us had to deal with most of the phone calls and meetings became angry, bitter, and stressed. The remaining spouse retained a glimmer of optimism. The tables clearly turned based upon who bore the responsibility for dealing with "the system."

Caseworkers held monthly vigil over a safety risk that discontinued to exist in our home. We never forgot how they turned tail on us when Daniel did major destruction to our house, refusing to help us maintain safety, yet insisted on inspecting our home monthly, once Daniel was gone, the house was repaired, and we were all safe. To add insult to injury, they continually complained about how over-worked they were and how they had too many cases to properly manage. When our other children were unsafe, DCFS closed their eyes. When we were all safe, they hovered over us like a dark cloud.

At the same time, we felt things ease up at home with Daniel not there. We had a little more freedom than we'd had in years past. We no longer needed to spend time fixing all the things that he broke. We didn't have to be hyper-vigilant anymore. We didn't worry every time a neighbor child strolled into our yard. We could relax, let our hair down a bit and enjoy spending some time any way we wanted to. It was liberating. Occasionally, we felt guilt about having it easier because that meant that other people had to deal our son, who was our responsibility.

And sometimes, I'd have a fleeting thought that it would just be easier to chuck it all and just give up. But within seconds, I'd see that pudgy faced little blue-eyed, blonde-haired boy who pressed each of his little hands on my cheeks, kiss me and say, "You pretty Mom!" I'd remember when he was two years old, telling him that I'd be his Mommy for whatever period of time he needed me to be and committing to him when he was four years old to be his mother for a lifetime. Any thoughts of giving up, faded quickly to black.

And as much as the therapists were trying to teach him to trust, so that he could let his guard down, our trust of people within the system waned by the day. By the third year, there wasn't any left. We'd long shared everything good and bad with our son's therapists. Initially, we wanted them to have every bit of information they'd need to help him heal. But, the longer the ordeal lasted, the more we started to put our guard up. We shared enough of ourselves to help Daniel, but there were some things we never even told the therapists. We'd laid so much of ourselves bare, and a lot of it had been used to attack us. We needed to reserve some sense of ourselves just for us, a part that we didn't have to share with "the team."

While everyone involved was trying to sell us that they were "helping" us, in essence we still felt like we were walking around with a gigantic target on our backs. No-fault dependency is a toned-down version of an abuse or neglect case.

Chapter Fourteen

SECONDARY STRESS: THRICE TRAUMATIZED

FROM PERSONAL EXPERIENCE, SECONDARY stress can creep up on someone completely unnoticed. Over time, we were thrice traumatized. First, we dealt with Daniel's trauma just as he did, solely by having him live in our home as our family member. Second, we were traumatized by numerous failed attempts at obtaining funding for his treatment, and third, in dealing with systematic oppression forced upon us by the child welfare and juvenile justice systems.

Trauma #1: Living With a Traumatized Child

At the initial clinical staffing, we faced a crossroads. We'd been forced into choosing between an illegal thing and an irresponsible thing. During that staffing, our therapist, Ronald, said something that caught me by surprise. He announced to the others in the meeting that Daniel's issues had created a secondary trauma within our family. For a moment, I was stupefied. Yes, this was hard, but I thought we were dealing with it as well as anyone does. Weren't we? Or did he see something that we could not?

Relative to psychological issues, the term trauma refers to anything that causes psychological pain or injury. Ronald was suggesting that we fell into this category as well, but for different reasons.

Daniel had indeed caused incalculable damage to our home. But it was nothing compared to the emotional damage he did to our family. Our other children were terrorized. We had four teens in our home, who were already dealing with normal hormonal fluctuations and teen drama. In addition, they were dealing with daily turmoil and upset due to Daniel's trauma, which included constant screaming, deliberate defiance, throwing objects, and chronic emotional upheaval. We had lived in a state of constant crisis for years. I was so stressed out; I wasn't even sleeping at night.

Jim and I were always waiting for the other shoe to drop. We had tried every behavior and treatment plan known to mankind and all of it failed. Daniel would agree to put the plan into practice, but the minute the counselor was out of sight, it all went out the window. Even in outpatient settings, after being in therapy all day long, Daniel was abusive. No sooner did the door close behind him, that he'd be swearing at us and throwing things at us in the car, turning the steering wheel while we were driving in an attempt to steer us into oncoming traffic.

We began to isolate ourselves. We'd show up to parties late and leave early, or one of us would stay home with Daniel. We'd had too many close calls with meltdowns at family gatherings and in other settings. We scaled back holidays. Even our dog was traumatized. When Daniel would go off on a rampage, poor Riley would hang his head and walk out of the room to hide until it was over.

And some memories flooded us at later dates. Getting out the Christmas decorations and realizing that we needed to buy some new ornaments. Daniel had flung the Christmas tree across the room and had broken most of them. We stopped buying Easter and Thanksgiving decorations. We couldn't leave anything sitting out. He was likely to use it as a shot-put. We were spent. We were broken. The well was completely dry. Perhaps it was the "dry well syndrome" that caused us not to succeed in obtaining funding for his treatment before being forced to trade custody. We were simply too spent to explore all the options. There was no one to help us who had the knowledge and expertise of navigating a very complex mental health system.

Even though I thought I was dealing with things well, it was seeing a photograph of me at a party that made me realize how stressed I'd become. My daughter had purchased a tanning package at a salon. She exited from her first visit with overall sunburn and decided that tanning packages weren't such a great idea for a fair-skinned Irish girl. Since she had several sessions left, I decided to give it a try. The tiny room was a mini-tropical paradise with its palm tree mirror and wicker chair. I lay down on that tanning bed, donned protective eyewear, positioned the headphones over my ears, and shut the lid. I listened to the soothing tropical music as the warmth engulfed my body. Ten minutes later, I was startled as the machine abruptly shut off, waking me from a sound sleep. As I lifted the lid and sat up, I couldn't believe how quickly I fell asleep. It was the best power nap ever. This was bliss! I returned to the salon over and over.

My daughter grew concerned about my repeated treks to the salon for my tanning naps. She cautioned me that I was placing myself at risk for skin cancer. Additionally, she worried that I was becoming addicted to tanning and would not be able to stop, placing me at even higher risk for skin cancer. She urged me to stop going. When I looked in the mirror, it was plain to see that I had a well-developed tan, but I didn't perceive it any differently than anyone else who spent time at beaches or on boats. That is, until I saw a photo of myself amongst my friends.

Randie celebrated her 50th birthday in the midst of our ordeal. She chose to celebrate her birthday at a luncheon with all of her best girlfriends. We had a photo taken of all of us that day. Weeks after the party, she gave me a copy of our group photo. I was shocked when I saw myself. Randie takes regular vacations to Florida and the Caribbean, so she is fairly tan, even in the winter. Standing next to me, she was pale by comparison. What had I done to myself?

About the same time, Daniel had been in the residential center for a few months and things were calming down at home. I returned to the tanning salon to finish up the last of the package. Once again, I lay down in my mini-paradise, complete with eyewear and headphones to wait for the heat wave and the Sandman. I enjoyed the music, but the Sandman never came. I popped the lid and sat up. Why hadn't I fallen asleep? I *always* slept in the tanning booth. The revelation hit me like a ton of bricks. Ronald's words besieged me again. "There is a secondary trauma within the family." I hadn't fallen asleep because I simply wasn't tired. I wasn't addicted to tanning. I hadn't gone to achieve a healthy glow. I went there to go to sleep. Once the stress left, I started sleeping at night like the rest of the world.

Trauma #2: The Funding Source Maze

The mental health system in Illinois is so complex and so broken that seasoned professionals have trouble navigating it. For an unwitting consumer to tackle it without guidance from a mental healthcare systems pilot, is overwhelming and unproductive.

SASS instructed us to apply for the Individualized Care Grant. They also told us everyone's first application is turned down automatically. Ours was. We were encouraged to appeal it. We did. When we pondered the reason for the denial, we realized that it was a futile attempt anyway. "Failure to meet criteria for impaired reality testing." We would learn that this was the most common reason for denial. Since our son was not hearing things that weren't there or seeing things that didn't exist, he would never meet this criteria anyway. It was a complete dead end. Why were they making us fill out this ream of paper repeatedly, just to be categorically denied? We also called DCFS Post Adopt to see if they could help us. They politely said no. We called our family insurance provider who told us there was not one dollar for residential coverage under our plan. We also called the number on Daniel's Medicaid card and were denied once again. We asked over and over again, how in the world do parents get their child into residential care anyway? We heard rumblings about getting the school to pay for it, but no one could tell us exactly how to make it happen. Our school seemed to think he was fine and that he problem was with us anyway. Each financial dead-end left us feeling increasingly helpless, frustrated, and traumatized. We were been twice traumatized before Dan ever entered residential treatment. Unbeknownst to us, we were headed for round three.

Trauma #3: Systematic Traumatization

We survived living with a traumatized child. We lost the battle for funding, but we survived a DCFS investigation, fighting back to clear our names. Daniel was now in a residential center.

With Daniel living elsewhere, as a family, we were finding a new normal at home. Over time, we stopped snapping at each other and started talking again. The laughter returned. We re-established relationships that were stronger and better. As the stress from living with a traumatized child began to dissipate, another type of stress was forming. The cause was the constant monitoring by case management and the judicial systems. I developed physical ailments that I never had before.

I had issues with neck and arm pain as well as migraine headaches that sent me running to the emergency room. It was uncharacteristic for me to have so many physical ailments for someone who is generally healthy and hesitates to take a pill for a headache. I always considered keeping busy a good way to forget about physical pain. I made a decision to use my new-found free time to finally do something for just for me.

I went to college. It was something I never had a chance to do when I was younger, but had always wanted badly. I found it to be a healthy coping mechanism. While it was much harder to go to college in my 40's than it would have been much earlier, studying my lessons, completing assignments, and taking tests forced me to think about something other than Daniel. At the end of four years, I had achieved a B.A. in Communications from Thomas Edison State College and was also awarded the Arnold Fletcher Award. Simultaneously, I'd earned my CISR insurance designation. I achieved some of my most important goals while a big part of my life was falling apart. Work and school forced me to think about something else and while they added to my load, in many ways, they provided an essential mental and emotional outlet. Without work, school, and Randie, I'm not sure I would have survived it all.

I could fill another book with stories of how the system beat us down. I share the one that netted the final showdown.

After the first residential center closed, Daniel was transferred to a facility downstate. While we disliked that it was 5 ½ hours away, we were convinced that this was the perfect facility for him. They understood trauma and they had a high success ratio for returning kids back home successfully. Because of the distance, DCFS had assigned a different caseworker, local to the area where Daniel was residing. We had just spent three months battling DCFS to get him into this facility. I was excitedly eager to visit my son for the first time in this new facility. The new caseworker, Clark, was eager to meet me and paid me a surprise visit. I was not forewarned about this part of the visit and didn't anticipate it. I wasn't done licking my wounds from the recent unnecessary court battle and quickly became defensive and annoyed. My body language suggested that I was borderline ticked off. I was. My displeasure increased, when he informed me that he didn't have the file yet and knew nothing about the case, expecting me to explain it all to him. It was the last thing I wanted to do in that moment. Every rotten thing his organization had ever done to me came spewing out of my mouth like an active volcano. He assured me that he would treat the case on its own merits, as a no-fault dependency case. He tried to convince me that they did things differently there and would not treat us as abusive parents as others had been doing. Clark tried to redirect the conversation to no avail. It was just time for him to go. The residential center staff member gazed at the floor and bit his lip.

Later that day, the staff member confided in me that he was so appalled at all that DCFS had done to our family that likely, he wouldn't sleep that night. The staff member also told me that Daniel had asked him what he thought of me. He responded that he thought I was very nice. Daniel remarked, "She's tough, isn't she?" The staff member smiled at him and replied, "It's clear to me that your mother loves you very much and is willing to go to bat for you. *That* is what is clear to me!"

Given more time, I might have come around to Clark's way of thinking. However, at the first clinical staffing, his supervisor strode into the room and spouted off, "Are the parents cooperating?" spoken in true abuse/neglect form, just as they do in the courtroom where we are all but invisible. We confronted him about whether they intended to treat our case as a no-fault dependency case, or treat it like an abuse case after they swore they wouldn't. He responded with a quick apology and a myriad of excuses. They had too many cases. Those were phrases they said to everyone. None of that went well either. We all tried to move on as best we could. We were stuck with each other regardless. That particular incident marked an emotional turning point for me, in spite of the additional scar that it left.

Concession

My internal thinking succumbed to the notion that no one was ever going to treat this situation on its own merits. The best it would get was to swallow our pride, slap the duct tape on our mouths, and grieve about it privately. Perhaps if we expected to be treated as criminals and child abusers, we wouldn't be so wounded when it happened. Perhaps it would alleviate some of the oppression that we constantly felt. I resorted to plan B. Show up. Stay in the oppress box. Answer what was asked. I would only have something to say, if there was something going on that affected Daniel negatively. After all, though they'd never openly admit it, it was clearly what they'd wanted from me all along. While I conceded that things were not going to change; I never stopped disliking it.

My emotional shift did not go unnoticed by the Family Service Coordinator at the residential center. She told us that she'd seen this before. We had been traumatized by the system causing us to be overly sensitive to DCFS' remarks. She remarked that trauma does not go away unless it's been processed. She recommended that Jim and I receive treatment for trauma.

We have known other parents with traumatized children, who have gone for therapy and/or medications to deal with their children's behaviors, and DCFS had used it against them, trying to portray them as weak, drug addicted, or just plain bad parents. We would not fall prey to another of their schemes. Our son was stuck in a system he didn't belong in and we were being processed through the child welfare management system as abusive and neglectful parents. For three years, we'd been subject to being constantly criticized, observed, monitored, evaluated, scrutinized, questioned, interrogated, investigated, inspected, humiliated, degraded, and dehumanized. We'd had enough! While our file may display "no-fault dependency," by virtue of DCFS processing us through the system as criminals, it was still a muted abuse case.

Our ultimate decision was to refuse trauma treatment. We asked the Family Service Coordinator to please relay to DCFS that if they were truly concerned about our traumatization, perhaps they could simply stop traumatizing us. At least give us enough time in between battles to lick our wounds before we had to face the next battle. Individually, we all found ways to cope. I channeled mine into advocacy.

The trauma in dealing with the system and our son's mental illness caused all of us to suffer physically, mentally, emotionally, and spiritually. In the end, it brought out the best and worst in every one of us.

"When children ran, they always ran home."

Karl Dennis

Chapter Fifteen

THE ADOPTIVE AND SAFE FAMILIES ACT

IN WATCHING THE FOSTER CARE population swell during the 1990's, public officials were bothered by the fact that kids stayed in foster care too long. Being activist minded, it's always great that people are bothered enough to take action. At the same time, what seems like a great idea at the time; sometimes creates unintended consequences over the long term. That is exactly what happened with the Adoptive and Safe Families Act of 1997, which was the brainchild of President Clinton and First Lady Hillary Clinton. This Act, along with the ones that preceded it, had longitudinal effects on children, parents, and state governments.

So, just how did so many kids end up in foster care anyway? Let's rewind a little further, back to another acronym: CAPTA or Child Abuse and Prevention Treatment Act. Commonly known as the Mondale Act, it created mandated reporters. It requires teachers and other childcare related professionals to report suspicions of neglect or abuse. This act had an unintended consequence called foster care panics. The states began taking too many children away from their parents, far too often and for too little cause.

National Coalition for Child Protection Reform advocate, Richard Wexler, has more of the answers. In his paper "Take the Child and Run: Tales From the Age of ASFA," citing a Casey Family study, a national study, and an Indiana study, children were from 25% to 75% more likely to be physically or sexually abused in foster care than with their biological families, even if the environment wasn't stable.

He contrasts these statistics with states that have used family preservation models including Michigan, Utah, Washington, California, North Carolina, and Minnesota. Wexler's report shows that children are safer when left in their birth families when preservation supports are in place, than they would have been in foster care. Wexler also cites a study from the University of Florida that compared the development of crack cocaine addicted babies raised by their birth mothers to addicted babies raised in foster care. The study showed that the babies raised by their birth mothers did better, proving that parent/child separation traumatizes children worse than living with a drug addicted parent.

What happened to the kids? In 1996, there were 30,000 more children still in the system than were adopted (Smith) rendering them legal orphans. They were traumatized by the initial allegations, separation from family members, and were often substance exposed as well. The abuse continued in foster care. It just happened by other people.

With so many children in foster care and not enough human services in place to help, federal and state governments made a push to move children from foster care into adoptive homes. ASFA was born in 1997 when President Clinton signed it into federal law.

ASFA's Original Goals

The Adoptive and Safe Families Act of 1997 was established with three goals and five principles in mind. The goals were:

1. Safety
2. Permanency
3. Well-being

The principles were as follows:

1. Safety is the paramount concern that must guide all child welfare services.
2. Foster care is temporary.
3. Permanency planning efforts should begin as soon as the child enters care.
4. The child welfare system must focus on results and accountability.
5. Innovative approaches are needed to achieve the goals of safety, permanency, and well-being.

Adoptions Increase

In 1997, President Clinton challenged states to double the number of adoptions within five years.

The Act created financial awards for states willing to increase numbers of adoptions. States received $4,000 for every finalized adoption and $6,000 for every special needs adoption. This presented an interesting financial challenge for the state of Illinois which had, more than 51,000 children in foster care, in 1997.

Illinois DCFS Director, Jess McDonald, jumped on board and met Clinton's goal in the first year. Adoption finalizations continued to rise and from 1996–2000, adoptions rose 78%. Illinois took the lead in Adoption Excellence Awards winning 5 of 18 awards in 2002 and 3 more awards in 2003. One of them was "One Church, One Child," in which African American churches encouraged one African American family per year to adopt an African American child.

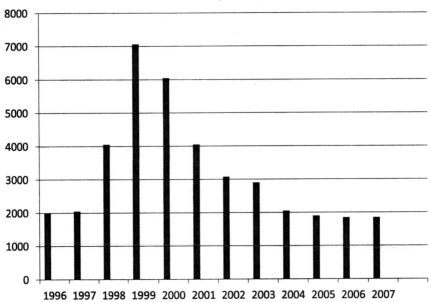

How did it work for the parents? In Illinois, DuPuy vs. Samuels proved that 75% of child abuse and neglect cases were overturned on appeal. The parents were never guilty. Children are still being confiscated from their parents without cause, manifesting in separation anxiety and post-traumatic stress in children. Imprisoned mothers had their parental rights terminated while awaiting trial. Even if they could get out of jail in time to regain custody of their children, they weren't given enough time to get back on their feet to regain custody of their children (Smith). Poverty stricken mothers and battered women also face charges of abuse and neglect rather than receive help. Regardless of the reason, children face the additional trauma of being separated from their parents.

So, what about the adopted kids? 50% to 75% have behavioral disorders and 1/3 have severe emotional disorders (CWLA 2009). Some of them kept their new families and adjusted fine. For others, diagnoses of mental and emotional disorders were overlooked, favoring labels of behavior disorders and juvenile delinquency. Kids who needed mental health services ended up in juvenile detention. Adoptive parents who got the diagnoses correct and protected their emotionally disordered children from juvenile detention wound up in a Catch 22. They couldn't get mental health services unless they were willing to make the "Devil's Deal"—trade custody rights for mental healthcare. The child would go through the child welfare horror for the second time in his life. The state makes the "Devil's Deal" too. They trade a child's sense of security and permanency for federal funding.

The ASFA Generation Enters Puberty

While the system did a great job at recruiting adoptive families, it failed to provide for the long term needs of children who'd been severely traumatized in infancy and early childhood, at a crucial stage of development. Thirteen years later, a host of acronyms were being labeled on most of the children who'd been adopted: ADD, ADHD, PTSD, ODD, RAD, OCD, CD, BD, and more.

Children who were severely neglected couldn't bond or attach well with their new parents, if at all. Many of them had altered brain chemistry because of pre-natal substance abuse affect. Thousands more suffered physical abuse as infants and toddlers. CWLA also reports that mental, emotional, and behavioral disorders have a direct correlation with trauma due to being placed with strangers, as well as impermanence resulting from multiple foster home moves.

Thirteen years later, numerous children began re-entering the system because the system didn't reach far enough for those children whose behavior could not safely be managed in a family setting, due to pre-adoptive trauma. Parents found themselves out of their leagues in caring for them at home, and were completely out of the ballpark in accessing funding to pay for it.

The *federal* government *gives permanency* under ASFA.
The *state* governments *take it away* in exchange for treatment.

Families Hit the Wall

Several early factors contribute to emotional regression and family burnout, over time. Community mental health departments lack funding for resources, as well as crucial interface and synergy with state agencies.

Lack of service delivery to families in their homes during the early stages of child emotional disregulation feeds impending crises. Over time, the child's behavior worsens and the family wears down. By the time the child's therapist recommends residential therapy, the family sits at the front gate applying for funding, not knowing that it can take a year or more to even open the gate to funding for residential care. When time runs out and the gate remains closed, there is only one option left. The key to unlocking the gate must be traded for the civil rights that parents hold most precious-the right to parent and make decisions for their children.

In fiscal year 2001, nationally, over 12,700 children who became wards either entered the juvenile justice system or became wards of the state because outpatient services failed to treat them sufficiently in out-patient settings. According to the 2003 Government Accountability Office Report, the children came from all economic levels and inflicted debilitating hardship on their parents and siblings, stressing them to the point that it strained them financially beyond their means and destroyed otherwise healthy family relationships. This number is likely small due to the states with the largest numbers of children not reporting at all. States with smaller numbers of children also failed to report.

Nebraska Safe Haven Debacle

On February 13, 2008, Nebraska Governor Heineman signed Legislative Bill 157, Safe Haven, into law in the 2008 Legislative Session. Forty-eight senators voted in favor of it. Nebraska was the last of the fifty states to enact a Safe Haven Law, in which a parent could abandon a child without fear of being charged with neglect or abandonment. Prior to the law being passed, legislators debated heavily about where to set the bar regarding the age limit. They did not reach a conclusive age, so they passed the law without an exclusionary age provision, stating, "No person shall be prosecuted for any crime based solely upon the act of leaving a child in the custody of an employee on duty at a hospital licensed by the state of Nebraska. The hospital shall promptly contact appropriate authorities to take custody of the child."

While the law was designed for safe infant abandonment, families with severely mentally ill children saw this as a way to get help for their children without fear of being charged with neglect. Parents began dropping off adolescent children at hospitals in order to access mental healthcare. Soon families from other states caught on and they also began bringing their mentally ill children to Nebraska under the Safe Haven Law.

Out of fear of becoming the safety net for the rest of the nation's mentally ill children, Nebraska legislators moved quickly, signing LB1 into law in a Special Session of the Legislature. LB1 limited the age of infant abandonment under the Safe Haven law to age 30 days or less. Forty-three senators voted for the final bill and Governor Heineman signed it into law on November 21, 2008.

By the time it was over, 36 children had been dropped off at Nebraska hospitals. There were some interesting demographics among them.

This set of statistics is hardly an exhaustive study, but it does shed some light on the family with a mentally ill child, who was unable to access mental health services and was burned out to the point of exhaustion. They were primarily Caucasian, single parent homes in urban areas, with a mentally ill child, and had a history of child welfare involvement.

The children were all teens, most from single parent homes. Hailing primarily from urban areas, out-patient mental health services were available. Nearly all families had used them and a third had required intensive services, higher than out-patient level.

There were twice as many Caucasian youth as African American youth. The North Carolina Social Services publication "Practice Notes" published an article called "African American Children in Foster Care," which calls attention to studies that show the ways in which African American families are discriminated against. Child welfare officials are more likely to remove children from African American parents, provide them with fewer services, and more quickly terminate their rights than Caucasian parents. When we couple those studies with the Nebraska Safe Haven statistics, it stands to reason that African American parents would fear social services more than dealing with severe mental health issues on their own.

Nebraska Safe Haven Statistics	# children
Caucasian	24
African American	11
Native American	1
From urban areas	33
Single parent home	32
Under 10 yrs. old	6
10-12 yrs. old	8
Over 13 yrs. old	22
Prior mental health services	34
Greater than outpatient mental health	12
Prior neglect/abuse allegations	34
Assessed safe from immediate harm	36
Current or previous state wards	20
Adopted/Relative/Guardianship placement	14
Medicaid eligible*	26

All 26 Medicaid eligible children were legally entitled to mental health services under the Early, Periodic, Screening, Diagnostic, and Treatment provision of Medicaid and were denied care at the same hospital where they were dropped off.

It is curious that almost all had prior allegations of abuse or neglect. The report did not explain the reasons for the allegations or whether they were indicated or unfounded. From my personal dealings with parents, I do know that some of their children sustained injuries when parents attempted to restrain kids or protect themselves from the child hurting them during a mental health rage. Others had children who falsely accused them of abuse while they were psychotic. Still others were reported to child protective services by a third party and children were "coached" into saying their parents abused them. Because this statistic in relation to this report is unclear, in my opinion, it is inconclusive and irrelevant. Regarding all the children being assessed as safe from immediate harm, mentally ill children are not violent and aggressive 100% of the time. It was likely easier to get the child to the hospital during a non-crisis period.

Thirty-four of thirty-six children were foster-adopt children with mental illness. *Thirty-four children became second time foster children during the Nebraska Safe Haven debacle.*

Almost three fourths of them had Medicaid. They were legally entitled to medically necessary services to correct or ameliorate their mental health conditions under the EPSDT provision of Medicaid. They were sent away by the people and institution charged with helping them under that provision. I further explain EPSDT in the next chapter on Solutions.

Illinois' Broken System

Do you remember when you were a small child and you wanted to ask permission for something and your mother said, "Ask your father," and your father said, "Ask your mother," leaving you without an answer? That's pretty much the approach in asking for mental health services in Illinois. Parents apply for ICG, who sends them to the school, who sends them to the Advocacy department, who sends them to the Mental Health Collaborative, who sends them to DCFS, who sends them back to the beginning to be denied all over again.

State and local funding resources vary from state to state. In Illinois, there are three tickets through the magic gate to residential care. If you don't get a ticket, head to the back of the line. If a parent had someone to help them navigate the lock, they'd get a heads up that they need to blitz them all at the same time. Most local mental health agencies in Illinois make two mistakes. They only tell them to apply for the Individualized Care Grant (ICG) and they don't advise them to contact the best kept secret in the state, Community and Residential Services Authority (CRSA). Unless they contact a special education attorney, they may not know that they may also apply for services through their school district or through DCFS clinical. It's a dark and murky path to the key that opens the gate to finding services that help.

Local mental health authorities can aid families in applying for the Individualized Care Grant, however, almost all families are turned down upon the first application. When they are turned down, they may file two appeals. After that, they must reapply. I have mentioned that the most common reason for ICG denials is "failure to meet impaired reality testing." Part of the criteria under Illinois Department of Health Services includes "Symptoms must include severely impaired reality testing and may include hallucinations, delusions, avoidance or withdrawal from human contact, marked affective instability, apathy, bizarre behavior, deficient or unusual forms of communication, agitation and/or danger to self or others." The statistics of those who are granted the ICG are slim. As of 2010, parents who were granted an ICG faced closed doors to finding services that accepted it. The state of Illinois became so far behind in their bills, service providers either refused to accept ICG, or closed their doors due to insolvency after a long stance of not being paid by the Department of Human Services.

According to Illinois Mental Health Planning and Advisory Council in 2009, 32% of the ICG applicants were adoptive children. The Individual Care Grant Program fiscal year 2009 report shows that in 2009, 807 families applied for the grant, 255 applications were reviewed, a paltry 48 applications were approved, leaving 759 families without medically prescribed services. In speaking with many families in person, many never applied for the grant at all because of the low probability of getting it. Thus, the number of applicants is likely much lower than the true need reflects.

On a personal note, we were one of those families, who waited to apply for it when we were stressed beyond normal functioning, because we kept hearing that we would not get it anyway. In retrospect, we wished we had applied for it sooner than we did. We'd heard rumblings that we might be able to get funding through our school district, but we had a few problems there too.

First, while some people had a general idea that residential treatment could be paid for by the school, no one seemed to be able to tell us exactly how to do it. We were too stressed to realize we needed a special education attorney. The school systems also have an application and appeal process. If that process fails, parents can sue the school district. However the process can take upwards of a year and cost tens of thousands of dollars. Once again, by the time parents have reached this juncture, they are emotionally and financially spent.

DCFS Post-Adopt children may also notify the department and ask for assistance. Once again, their process is generally discovered and applied for after the family has thrown in the towel in believing they will never access appropriate treatment. It takes months to even get an appointment, months more in waiting for a decision, and there is always a chance of complete denial. Even if parents are successful at this juncture, the duration of services is limited. In most cases the child will not stabilize before this funding source ends. If a parent applies through DCFS, waits a year, then applies for ICG and waits a few more, then has to sue the school district for another year; the child is practically grown before they ever get a funding source for treatment.

As resource after resource fails, families are being encouraged to seek safety for themselves and their family members by relinquishing custody rights for mental healthcare, by mental health professionals who are unable to help the children on an out-patient basis. In short order, out-patient services are exhausted. The child's condition becomes increasingly violent and dangerous and in order to protect themselves, they are left with four brutal choices, each with its own equally brutal consequence.

Which Would You Choose?

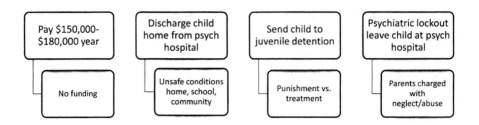

Re-evaluating ASFA Goals

A generation of ASFA kids are now in their teens. Just how well did this federal act serve them and the families who love them? Let's take a new look the goals and principals that defined it.

Safety

Factor safety as it pertains to the child, his siblings, parents and other household family members. In considering safety, let's look at who remains safe before as well as after a relinquishment occurs.

Prior to relinquishment, the child's behavior is unmanageable and he is unsafe. He may be hurting himself physically to gain attention. His own actions may cause danger to himself. The damage he does to others brings consequence upon himself. The family and other household family members are unsafe. They are being physically and emotionally attacked in their home, possibly including threats of being killed. The community is not safe either. Children coming to the child's house to play or visit and other students at school and in the community are also at risk of harm.

After relinquishment, the child is safe. The family and other members are safe, and so is the community. It took the parents losing custody to make everyone safe.

Permanency

Prior to relinquishment the child has a strong sense of permanency. Adoption is forever. In forcing parents into a situation where they have no choice but to trade custody for services, the very same people who taught the child that their new family was permanent, are now teaching him that the same family is dispensable. Permanency can be disrupted or even dissolved based upon how serious and financially intensive his mental health needs are. What is given on one hand is taken away with the other.

Well-Being

Prior to the relinquishment, the child has a sense of belonging and well-being. However, the family, household members, and the community do not have a sense of well-being. They are wrought with upset and fear. After the relinquishment, the child does not have a sense of well-being. He is in the hands of strangers, separate from a loving family. The system processes him through as if he were an abused child, traumatizing him further. After the relinquishment, the family and household members can feel safe from harm, however, they don't have a sense of well-being because they are now dragged through courts as abusers. Separated from their loved one, they have lost the family intimacy that goes along with remaining united as family members.

The child meets the goals prior to relinquishment even when he is in severe crisis. After relinquishment, he loses his sense of permanency and well-being. The landscape looks very different for the family members. Prior to relinquishment they are not safe or well, but they retain a sense of permanency. After the relinquishment, they trade a sense of safety for the loss of permanency, and are not well either before or after relinquishment.

We can conclude that the only way for ASFA to maintain the original goals of safety, permanency, and well-being for child and family, is to provide treatment for the child in a setting which keeps everyone safe and preserves permanency.

Did ASFA succeed in meeting its goals?	Child	Family
Prior to Relinquishment		
Safety	YES	NO
Permanency	YES	YES
Well Being	YES	NO
After Relinquishment		
Safety	YES	YES
Permanency	NO	NO
Well Being	NO	NO

Re-evaluating ASFA Principles

We have resolved that ASFA failed to meet the original goals. Did the five guiding principles fare any better?

1. *Safety is the paramount concern that must guide all child welfare services.*

   Many foster-adopt children were pre-adoptively exposed to drugs, alcohol, sex, and violence. Many were neglected at a critical stage of development. These experiences damaged their brains, causing severe emotional and behavioral disorders which manifested in dangerous societal behaviors. Post-Adopt provides adoption preservation and directs families to out-patient services, but there is no clear cut path for families requiring more intensive services.

   Child welfare services fail to use safety as a guide for situations which result in psychiatric lockouts which lead to adoption disruption and dissolution. There is no safety net which provides for safety, concurrent with family preservation.

2. *Foster care is temporary.*

   Children need stable, loving, and consistent family homes to provide the right environment for healthy physical, social, and emotional growth and development during the formative years. Foster care was developed as a way of providing care for children who needed a temporary living environment until they could return home to their birth families or become adopted by another family. It was intended to be temporary.

   By governments either actively promoting relinquishment or failing to establish a path for avoiding it, they send a clear message to children that foster care is not temporary, but episodic.

   If we didn't want children languishing in foster care the first tour, we should be even more concerned about returning them to the same system for a second tour.

3. *Permanency efforts should begin as soon as the child enters care*

   Adoption preservation services are available on a limited basis for those who ask for them. Families find themselves out of their leagues when they have exhausted every available out-patient service and are still living with a dangerous child. Strong permanency efforts should begin as soon as the severity of the child's mental health disorders becomes known. Parents need access to intensive services and treatment to support permanency. They need emotional and moral support from their child's treatment team.

They don't need to be attacked, ridiculed or blamed by anyone in clinical, child welfare, or juvenile justice systems. Parents feel they are fighting on too many fronts. They feel the pressure of dealing with a mentally ill child, the pressure of funding and accessibility of services, and the pressure of a system that works against them.

Permanency efforts begin, but they don't go far enough for the most critically ill children, dropping them through the hatch, and destroying permanency.

4. *The child welfare system should focus on results and accountability*

The child welfare system does not even track how many children are re-entering the system because of unmet clinical needs for mental and behavioral healthcare. There is no synergy between state departments. Trying to access intensive care is like aiming a gun at a moving target. Hit or miss. No one state department, state agency, or organization is assigned responsibility for results and accountability for adoption preservation.

5. *Innovative approaches are needed to achieve safety, permanency, and well-being*

Now that the ASFA generation is in their teens, I re-evaluate the three goals and five principles that formed the Adoptive and Safe Families Act of 1997. I deduce that ASFA has failed children and their families on all of its goals and principals.

States were given financial incentives to increase adoptions. The ASFA generation makes it clear that the states also need financial incentives to preserve adoptions. States need to grab the baton from the federal governments and make sure that adoptive children and their families are able to maintain safety, permanency, and well-being until the child reaches majority status.

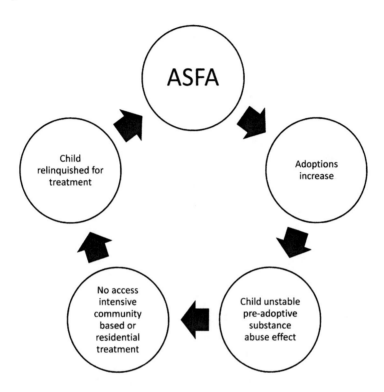

When allegations are founded and children really are unsafe at home, they may enter the child welfare system. When they are unable to return home, for those who are fortunate enough to be adopted, the cycle should be complete. For those with serious emotional or behavioral disturbances due to pre-adoptive trauma, the cycle continues; they re-enter the system and the cycle begins all over again.

According to a report of the Screening, Assessment, and Support Services in Illinois, there were 104 psychiatric lockouts in 2010, up from 27 in 2004, and rising steadily since 2007. That is about one per county.

The original intents and purposes of ASFA are defeated when adoptions are disrupted due to the circumstances which brought them into the system the first time.

Chapter Sixteen

SOLUTIONS

HOW CAN THE PROBLEM OF custody relinquishment for mental healthcare be solved? As is true for most complex problems, there are a variety of solutions available. Parents in other states have successfully tackled this problem, by working together with, fighting against, and when necessary, suing their state governments. By identifying the problem, analyzing the solution, giving it scope, pulling in available resources, and resolving to make it a win/win situation for all, change can happen. I don't claim to have all the answers, but a good start is with EPSDT, Voluntary Placement Agreement, and the Katie Beckett option.

Federal or State?

When I first dissected the problem of custody relinquishment, I had to consider which government to work with. Was this a federal problem or a state problem? The answer is both. Primarily it is a state issue which is why the problem exists in some states and not others. The states have the bulk of the problem for assigning (or failing to assign) funding. The federal government aids and hinders the problem by providing options, which states may utilize according to their discretion and disposal. The most comprehensive law falls under a federal Medicaid provision called the Early, Periodic, Screening, Diagnostic, and Treatment (EPSDT), which is an entitlement.

Scope

A mini-social services history lesson gives us a little history and a bigger scope. For the purpose of understanding EPSDT, we don't need to go back to World War I, but it never hurts to preface any given law with a little background.

What do we know about EPSDT? It was passed in 1967 with the goal of discovering and addressing children's medical needs early on, so that problems would not go undetected and uncorrected, causing more extensive problems in later developmental stages.

What precipitated it? The Social Security Act.

What was the driving force behind the Social Security Act? The Great Depression, which began in 1929 and lasted until the late 1930's. In 1932, President Franklin D. Roosevelt won the election by promising the people a "new deal," in response to the Great Depression. The New Deal, as it has been proclaimed in our history, was based upon the premises of relief, recovery, and reform.

What else was going on in the world at that time?

- The United States was recovering from massive bank failures and the fallout from Black Friday, the Wall Street crash.
- 1935—Germany, Heinrich Himmler developed a program for breeding an Aryan "super race."
- Amelia Earhart flew solo across the Pacific Ocean
- The first public housing project was launched in New York

While each one of those events denotes individual merit, collectively, they paint a broad stroke of the social and political landscape of that era. During his tenure, President Roosevelt instituted a host of social reform laws, including the Social Security Act. During that time, Social Security held a much different context. It was a governmental savior for the unemployed, the hungry, and the poor. It was "social insurance," paid upfront and collected on the back end in time of serious need.

EPSDT

Today, the mention of Social Security holds an entirely different context. For most people, it's an indeterminate and unquestioned sum of money the government takes out of our paychecks that we don't expect to see until a future time in which we become disabled or retired. In truth, there are many components to it and it encompasses much more than most people realize.

Social security benefits are administered by the Health Resources and Services Administration in Washington D.C. Between 1967 and 1989, Congress amended a number of laws within Title V of the Social Security Act. EPSDT was one of the first.

EPSDT is the child health component in federal Medicaid. According to the United States Department of Health and Human Services, "Since 1967, the purpose of the EPSDT program has been 'to discover, as early as possible, the ills that handicap our children and to provide continuing follow up and treatment so that handicaps do not go neglected.' Federal law – including statutes, regulations, and guidelines – requires that Medicaid cover a very comprehensive set of benefits and services for children, different from adult benefits. Since one in three U.S. children under age six is eligible for Medicaid, EPSDT offers a very important way to ensure that young children receive appropriate health, mental health, and developmental services."

EPSDT states in part, that if a practitioner of the healing arts deems that a treatment is medically necessary, to correct or ameliorate a condition, the state must provide it, whether or not it is covered under any other state plan. If the state cannot provide it, it must arrange for it. In Illinois, as well as in other states, the government tries to limit the statute. For example, the parent might be required to apply for other types of state aid and exhaust all other funding possibilities and being forced to relinquish custody rights without ever having a discussion about the EPSDT provision of Medicaid.

EPSDT is an entitlement. It is not an option. There is no exception, exclusion, or condition which precludes this basic entitlement. It is what it is; an entitlement. When you begin to understand legal wording, you find a clear distinction within the statutes regarding the words "must" or "shall" and "may." If the statute includes the word "must" or "shall," the law is clear. It has to be done. There are no optional features or mild interpretation. It is cut and dry, black and white. "Must" and "shall" equal "required." When the law uses the word, "may," there is an option. It is not mandatory according to the law, but it is allowable by the law.

The EPSDT law seems pretty clear, right? If a treatment is medically necessary, the state *must* provide it. Some states mistakenly believe that it is optional. They make excuses that they don't have enough money, facilities, or providers. They have existing state rules which nullify the federal law. If no one impresses upon them that they are required to provide it; it's easy enough to leave well enough alone. It takes parents, advocacy groups, legislators, and grass roots campaigns to enforce federal compliance. Even once the state governments do understand it, they act slowly, if at all, to implement reform.

New Direction-EPSDT

Shortly after I joined NAMI, other members were pretty excited about an upcoming mental health court conference. A number of them planned to attend. I made some inquires about potential juvenile court seminars. I discovered there were none, although, after hearing about my issues, a woman did steer me towards another group that might like to hear about what I'd been working on. It was a conglomeration of mental health board presidents who'd formed their own alliance. They called it The Association for Community Mental Health Authorities of Illinois (ACMHAI). They shared with me their position paper on EPSDT. Because of my own research, I knew that NAMI and the Bazelon Center for Mental Health Law held EPSDT out as a solution for custody relinquishment. What I didn't know, was why Illinois was not implementing this federal mandate. ACMHAI had organized an EPSDT forum which was to be held the day prior to the mental health court conference. I accepted and invited other parents, advocates, and senate staff. They asked if they could open the meeting with my video, "He's My Son." I granted permission.

When I arrived, I learned just how many people were interested in EPSDT. Nearly every child mental health stakeholder in the state was present: state departments, providers, mental health attorneys, mental health advocacy groups, and ACMHAI members. The senator of my district sent some of his staff at my request. I brought other families with me and we passed out copies of the families' stories which outlined attempts and failures at obtaining funding for treatment, and also included how we were all being persecuted in exchange for our children's mental healthcare. Various people spoke and made presentations. A slide presentation outlined EPSDT in detail. Discussion followed regarding why this provision was not being applied in Illinois. A representative from Healthcare and Family Services noted that the residential treatment centers were not licensed as PRTF or psychiatric residential treatment facilities, which is why they could not bill Medicaid for services. Others asked if Illinois had any facilities licensed as PRTFs. Yes, some were, but they only accepted kids with substance abuse issues. Would they be willing to re-license the other centers as PRTF's? Perhaps. They'd check into it and circle back.

My presentation from the families was last. I explained that when parents could not obtain residential treatment for their children, they defaulted to DCFS case management and the juvenile court system, where we were being processed through their systems in the same manner as abusive parents. I described some of the details of our ordeal. The audience cringed. I explained how the Juvenile Court Act was not intended to be used for psychiatric lockouts. There were no existing laws that the judges could apply which didn't criminalize either parent or child. The feedback from that meeting was clear. The child mental health stakeholders agreed that the presentation with the most impact was the family stories. They could not sit on this any longer. It was time to take action.

I stayed connected with many of the ACMHAI members. CRSA also offered a fair amount of information and insight. We all waited to hear if HFS would agree to license the centers as PRTF's and heard nothing. ACMHAI organized a follow up EPSDT meeting.

Prior to that meeting, I was invited by two ACMHAI members to attend a meeting with Governor Quinn's senior health policy advisor at the

James R. Thompson Center at the governor's office in Chicago. I readily accepted. Governor Quinn became Governor by default, after former Governor Rod Blagojevich was impeached.

I recalled the last time I visited the James R. Thompson Center. Years prior, I had taken Samantha and Daniel there to perform Irish dance for then Governor Rod Blagojevich's Christmas tree lighting celebration. I remembered the 8 x 10 photo of the former governor, who posed with the costumed dancers after the performance. Rod had his arm around a handsome, 8 year old, Daniel.

Once we arrived at that meeting, the other women made a plea for expanding in-home and community based services under Medicaid's EPSDT provision, while I made the case for residential treatment. The health policy advisor was well acquainted with this law as he'd worked with it in the past. He was intrigued by their plans, but plagued by billions in state debt, due to the poor economy. We explained the licensing trouble. He'd speak with HFS to see what could be done and get back to us. His time was limited.

Because it was clear he was trying to maximize federal dollars, I tossed out an idea that I hadn't planned on presenting that day, in the hope that it might grab his attention. It did. I reminded him that the state was taking in large sums of money from the federal government for the purpose of increasing adoptions. Almost a third of adoptions were currently at risk of disruption or dissolution, due to inability to access residential care. If the federal government was giving us money to increase the numbers of adoptions, could they give us money to preserve them? "What?" he asked. I pulled the statistics from my briefcase which showed a list of states and how much federal money they'd gotten. Illinois' share was about a quarter million dollars. He compared the numbers and made comments about why other states had gotten more than Illinois. He asked if that was his copy. "Um, sure!" I said. It was during the final 15 seconds of that meeting that he asked me, "Why *did* you adopt those mentally ill kids anyway?"

I dared to hope that the center where Daniel was residing might be the first to be licensed as a PRTF. There was no word from HFS regarding the re-licensing any of them. They were dragging their feet.

I started making inquiries to law firms that specialized in class action lawsuits. A few of them expressed interest. We already had enough parents to file one. Attorneys were surprised at the depth of knowledge that I had on this issue. It might be the only way that we could get Daniel the care that he was legally entitled to and regain the custody we never should have lost.

About a month after the meeting at the governor's office, ACMHAI hosted the second EPSDT forum. The meeting began by asking an HFS representative for an update on the PRTF issue. He responded by saying that it would take time. They wanted to do it right. I asked him if they had a time frame for completing it. He answered that they had talked about it for over a decade and had no specific timeline. The Department of Alcohol and Substance Abuse confirmed that they'd been licensing their centers as PRTFs for the last 15 years.

I spoke up, "What you are saying is that if a child has a mental health issue *concurrent* with a substance abuse issue, the child gets treatment and the parents *retain* custody. But if a child has a mental health issue *void* of a substance abuse issue, the child gets treatment and the parents *lose* custody."

You could have heard a pin drop in that room. No one could contradict the statement I had just made. After HFS admitted they had no distinct timeframe for licensing residential centers as PRTFs, judging by the looks of the faces around the room; it was clear that the first person in Illinois to file a federal lawsuit for residential treatment under the EPSDT provision of Medicaid would likely be me. What no one knew was that there was an attorney just a few miles away from where that meeting was held, who just a few hours earlier, had agreed to represent our case.

The Governor's senior health policy advisor fielded a few questions that day without making any firm commitments. As he left the room, I handed him a copy of my white paper on the Adoptive and Safe Families Act and how children were recycling back into foster care. I also handed him a CD of "He's My Son." He accepted it with hesitation, asking me, "What is *this*?" I told him it was a copy of our story and I wanted him to watch it. He gazed at the floor. He couldn't make eye contact with me. He apologized sincerely for our family's anguish and walked out the door.

Reducing Costs with In-Home and Community Based Services

In-home and community based services bear less overall cost than expensive residential and other out of home placements. Expensive in-patient hospitals become the default providers when less intensive family and community supports are not available. States fear having enough state funds to cover their 32% portion of Medicaid costs. By using these less restrictive services when practical, intensive services are often avoided later on. The 32% of upfront cost is saved on the back end, by avoiding hospital and residential stays.

This is not to say that we should get rid of residential centers all together. Even with extensive wraparound programs, some kids' behaviors cannot be safely managed in a home setting. When children require residential treatment, they should receive it for the shortest time possible, with the ultimate goal of stabilization and return home. Besides the idea of saving on the front end, the states neglect to consider all the funds lost through unnecessary court costs and litigation.

When appropriate options are not extended to the child and family, and a lockout occurs, the case defaults to child welfare and juvenile court. The state's tax dollars are then put to work paying numerous caseworkers, state funded attorneys, and court costs. The state incurs massive amounts of money in defense costs when family advocates rise up and file suit against them. Even if we fail to consider that paying on the back end is penny wise and pound foolish, the true cost is paid through lack of the child's recovery and decreased relationship with his parents. This contributes to a child's perception of stigma to himself and his family.

If EPSDT is the answer for Medicaid eligible children, it is important not to leave a gaping hole for non-Medicaid eligible children. States can and should institute a safety net for the remaining children, lest any child be forced to trade parents for treatment. They are the Katie Beckett Option, or TEFRA, and Voluntary Placement Agreement.

TEFRA and Katie Beckett

Some states offer a waiver, called TEFRA, or Tax Equity and Fiscal Responsibility Act. This is also known as the Katie Beckett option. Katie

Beckett was a 3 year old girl, who was hospitalized in Iowa, for two years. As part of her medical treatment, she needed to be on a ventilator most of the day. Medicaid would pay for her treatment as long as she remained in the hospital. This was costing the government six times as much in medical costs. Her parents wanted her home, but they could not afford her treatments without the aid of Medicaid. While government officials turned a blind eye to the family's plight, then President Ronald Reagan stepped in. He called it "cold bureaucracy." He expressed outrage at a press conference calling for a change in Medicaid rules. The government responded positively. The same year, Katie Beckett was home by Christmas. While hospitalized, Katie's prognosis was bleak. Even her doctors said she'd be better off at home, being less exposed to bacteria and sickness, which are inherent in a hospital setting. Once home, she made substantial progress. Katie is now an adult and a healthcare advocate, along with her mother, who fought so hard for her care.

How are children who are taken from their families and relinquished in exchange for treatment, so different from Katie Beckett? State governments are spending tax dollars in court costs, unnecessarily criminalizing parents, when they could be saving that money and reapplying it towards intensive and residential treatment. By providing treatment, overall costs are less, children heal faster, and families are preserved. Still another viable option that has worked well in other states is the Voluntary Placement Agreement.

Voluntary Placement Agreement

The reason many state governments choose to take guardianship in place of treatment, is so that they can draw down Title IV funds from the federal government for having a child in foster care. The federal law states that in order to receive this funding the state must take responsibility for care and placement. The statute does not require care and custody. At the time of this writing, Illinois is one such state that misunderstands this statute and continues to force families to make the guardianship/funding trade-off. The risk in having a Voluntary Placement Agreement is that some states attach a child support clause, in which parents must make payments to the state for their child's care. Some parents report that the child support is also in excess of what they are able to afford, defeating the original purpose of the

Voluntary Placement Agreement. Reforming plans to meet family's needs offers the best solution. Results and accountability hold state departments accountable for system effectiveness and plan modifications.

Many states have found that implementing services under EPSDT, the Katie Beckett Option, and Voluntary Placement Agreement are solutions that have abolished custody relinquishment in their states. This doesn't mean there aren't other options. We cannot rely solely on the government to make wise choices for us. It is up to the people facing the issues to find the answers and advocate for change. Reviewing models that have worked in other states is one way, but it is important not to limit yourself. Think outside the box and when you have to, throw the box away. Plan with the end goal in mind. Advocate for whatever works.

"If you always do what you've always done, you'll always get what you've always got."

Anthony Robbins

Chapter Seventeen

CHANGING SYSTEMATIC RESPONSE

SYNERGY. REMEMBER THE HOCKEY lesson? The sum of the parts is greater than the whole. In viewing a clinical case through the abuse lens, the accepted conundrum is that each department works individually from every other department, when they should be working in tandem. In other words, they're all on separate pages and the entire book is so disconnected, it doesn't make the least bit of sense. It may stand to reason that the juvenile court works independently from DCFS, but even the departments within The Department, don't interface or communicate very well.

How did we get here:

Foster Child → Adopted Child → Adoption Preservation → Clinical → Investigations → Neglect Case → Dependency Case → Adoption Disruption

When we need to be here:

Foster Child → Adopted Child → Trauma treatment → Adoption Preservation

Let's watch the relay race from an organizational standpoint. The child is refused access to treatment due to lack of funding, forcing the family into a psychiatric lockout. Post-Adopt has failed to aid the family in identifying, applying for, and securing treatment for the child. Post-Adopt hands the baton to Clinical. Clinical has entered the scene when the child is too dangerous to return home and the family is too stressed to receive him home. Clinical passes the baton to Investigations. Investigation caseworkers are trained in neglect and abuse cases, so they treat the psychiatric lockout as such, charging and indicating the family with neglect or abuse. Investigations backhands one baton to Case Management and another to Juvenile Court. Case Management and Juvenile Court only have procedures and protocols for abusive and neglectful parents, so they treat no fault dependency exactly the same.

Navigators

How did things get so bad without anyone at DCFS being aware of it? Parents lack a clinical case manager or navigator who tells them when to apply for the Individualized Care Grant that too few get, or that they have to be turned down for, before getting anything else. They lack knowing when and how to ask the school district for funding and how to proceed with due process after being denied. CRSA is still the best kept secret in the state of Illinois; even though they can help when getting them involved early enough. When a child is being admitted to a psychiatric in-patient hospital repeatedly, Post-Adopt could assign a personal clinical case manager. This manager would help the family navigate intensive services while keeping everyone safe and offer support through the most stressful times, but currently, they don't.

Create a New Channel

Families need a separate channel within child welfare for mental healthcare services, one that does not include being investigated for a non-criminal matter. An alliance between DCFS Clinical and Adoption Preservation could easily set up a process that offers children and families the services and support they really need, while not wasting time and tax money on ones they don't want or need. The family knows the child and his needs best. Clinicians know that complex clinical cases should be *family driven* according to the family's wishes.

Alleviate Investigations

Hotline calls are intended for children who were neglected or abused. They were never intended for children for whom the government denied access and funding for intensive mental healthcare services. On the off chance that they got involved anyway, investigators are charged with the same things as any of us who work in business. They are licensed. They are mandated to take continuing education classes and be well-versed in their organization's policies. When in doubt, re-read the rules, double-check, and consult with superiors.

Acknowledge the Injustice

With regard to a psychiatric lockout in which a child re-enters the system after being denied access to mental healthcare, case management holds a double standard. Caseworkers are guilty of taking away the most precious gift the child ever received, his family. The gift that they take was the very same gift that another caseworker, assigned to the same child earlier in his life, was so excited to give.

Make a conscious effort to envision the parents as they are. Foster-adopt parents are long term child welfare advocates just like caseworkers. The difference is that parents accepted a lifetime role. These are the same parents who also wanted permanency for their child and badly desired to preserve that permanency. Avoid speaking to them and treating them as if they are abusive. Give them credit for the knowledge and wisdom they have gained along the way. Recognize that they are graduates in the School of Hard Knocks. Support the family. If you must be involved, be as invisible as possible. Encourage the child to obey and respect his parents. Don't drive a wedge between them. Don't assign an educational surrogate when the parents are fully capable of advocating for their child's educational needs. Educate judges, that unless there is a specific reason for appointing CASA, this child's "best interests" are served by the people who love him the most, his parents.

How different would it be if a child could get the services he needed with full support of his family? How different would it be to have his parents drive him to the residential facility, make his bed, and put his clothing in the drawers, rather than to have him picked up by a stranger, told his parents are in trouble, and whisked away to a place that is unfamiliar and far away? To have his loving parents make medical and legal decisions for him rather than an investigator, a caseworker, an attorney, an educational surrogate, a volunteer stranger, and a judge? In order to truly address the child's "best interests," the system must change. The people working within the system must move to the back seat and let the parents drive. They have a lot more experience with their child and they'll get into a lot less accidents.

Synergize. The sum of the parts is greater than the whole.

Chapter Eighteen

IMMORAL, UNETHICAL, ACCEPTABLE

A NEW LEADER SPRINGS up and sells a morally wrong and unethical idea to the general public, convincing them that the idea is not only acceptable, but is in the best interests of all people. The idea incubates and grows in a community environment, infecting people's values and morals.

The longer we endured our ordeal, the more oppressed we felt. I began to think a lot about the whole concept of oppression. What is the role of the victimizer? What is the role of the victim? How does it become socially acceptable on any level, let alone on such a grand scale? I began to draw a few similarities between the concentration camp victims, slaves, and those of us who were forced into making the Devil's Deal. The victimizers, using propaganda, all sold their barbaric plans to society, who got sucked into it. The victims were all counted and labeled with numbers. The oppression defined who they were during their captivity and the effects of their ordeal remained with them for a lifetime.

As I watched a short video of a Holocaust survivor telling his story, a Jewish man discussed how the term "stinkin' Jew" became so commonplace.

That phrase was repeated so often that people began to believe that it was true. It made me think of how often we were put down. To a lesser degree, Jim and I identified with being treated like a second class citizen. Though our ordeal doesn't parallel that of the Holocaust survivors, we began to feel like a lot like the "stinkin' parents."

Trading Custody Rights for Mental Healthcare

Intentionally or unintentionally, governmental state departments and juvenile justice systems are making mentally ill children legal orphans. They sell the "Devil's Deal" to each other, as well as to the families, as accepted protocol. Support for the philosophy is sold to the public by focusing on the "child's best interests." In truth, it is not the "child's best interests" at all, nor the least detrimental alternative, rather the option of last resort. It lands in child welfare and juvenile justice, completely by default. It is accepted because in the end, the child does obtain much needed treatment and the family doesn't lose all of their rights. They justify it by passing responsibility to other state departments and failing to pass laws to address it. It is less of an issue of actually addressing the problem, than it is lack of motivation to tackle such a complex, multi-systemic problem.

DCFS caseworkers are the instruments that deliver the bad news, take our children, and try to convince us they are helping us. They try to paint a picture of reunification when separation was never necessary to begin with, had the right thing been done from the start. We've been told we are bad parents. We've been charged with civil crimes that we did not commit. We've been separated from our son and forced to trade common civil liberties for mental healthcare. We've had to defend ourselves in two different courts and became the plaintiff in a third. We've been forced to cooperate under coercive verbal threats which we watched carried out against other families. We had to watch our son grieve, as he lost his family for the second time, due to the trauma that caused him to lose the first one, and which damaged the part of his brain that regulates his emotions. We've been placed in the same arena, in professional's minds, as well as physically in their offices and courtrooms, as parents who abused their children. Over a period of years, two local governmental systems also began to view us as the "stinkin' parents."

Bystanders and Secret Angels

Many parties stood by and watched it all go downhill. Our county mental health department saw our demise coming and didn't act early enough to help us prevent it. They failed to inform us of all the available options. We say the same for DCFS Adoption Preservation Services. Some of the private clinicians did what they were able, but they drew the line when supporting us meant risking their funding from the state departments. Hospital staff refused to retain our son, who was at risk of hurting others, for two more days so we could gain additional assistance and advice. Our school district failed to provide treatment under his Individualized Educational Plan. The state's attorney followed the law before him and gave us a heads up about the rough road we were about to tread. The GAL gave little credence to our role in our son's life. The DCFS Director, Advocacy office, and Governor's office ignored all of my pleas and inquiries.

As many people failed us, there were others who rescued us when we needed it and picked us up when we were down. One of our therapists repeated something so often, we began to believe it. "He will not get better without you." Thank you, Ronald. We always knew that, but it was helpful to be reminded on a regular basis.

Other clinicians kept in regular touch, asking how our son was, and checked in to see how we were dealing with things. Our families and friends were there when we needed them to be, but we felt even more support from other adoptive families. Other advocates kept our heart tanks filled with hope. When our main support system let us down, NAMI picked us up and helped us move forward. Through everything, there were two angels that really stand out as the true saviors—the judges and the attorneys.

The judges interpreted the law as best they could considering they didn't have laws to use which were appropriate to the situation. Unlike others, they treated us respectfully in court, and once in a while, even asked if we had anything to say, which meant the world to us. One of them even stretched her limits a bit to help us get our son into an appropriate treatment center. We are grateful for her ingenuity. We appreciate that no judge ever threatened us with complete termination of our parental rights.

While people working within the system found the whole process acceptable, people outside the system were stifled by their indifference. Attorneys, Aaron Rapier and Shawn Collins, from the Collins Law Firm believed in us and in adoption preservation. When I finally figured out the EPSDT laws and still couldn't get the state to pay for our son's care, Aaron listened to me explain a complicated story and eagerly developed a plan to help. Often, the two lawyers vocally and openly questioned why the state departments treated mentally ill children as damaged goods, refusing them care on equal terms with physically ill children. They wondered aloud how the state departments could blatantly refuse to obey a federal law and get away with it. Visibly disturbed, they offered to help us.

Numbered and Tallied

Those who suffer the most are mentally ill children and their parents, who get stuck in a system they don't even belong in. What should be treated as a mental health clinical case gets processed through child welfare and juvenile justice in the same manner as an abuse case. The longer the case continues, the deeper the systematic oppression towards the child and family. We don't need to be attacked or processed. We need support. The children are labeled with a court case number. It made me think of how the Jews were tattooed and the slaves were forced to wear a metal tag. As many times as I heard our son's number repeated in court, it was the day that the CASA volunteer referred to my son as his case number on my answering machine, that I put it all together. I still remember that day. I felt horrified, numb, and deeply saddened. If the children had to wear that number so that it was visible, would people in the system be bothered by it? Or would they desensitize to that as well, over time?

I began to think about how sorely immoral and unethical the Holocaust and slavery were. Custody relinquishment for mental healthcare is also. Yet, each was legal in its time, and society allowed each of them to be tolerated. I wished I had a dime for every time someone said to me, "That's just the way it is." The child welfare system believes that custody relinquishment is acceptable.

As I think about how so much of this is about money and how little of it is about the children, my mind often wanders to one of my favorite movies, "Schindler's List." I think of the scene near the end of the movie when the Nazi's are falling and Oskar Schindler tries to escape Krakow with his wife. Twelve hundred Jews appear to present him with a gift to thank him for saving their lives. Oskar's right hand man, Itzhak Stern, who became his friend, placed the gift in his palm. It was a ring that they'd made using a gold filling from one of the detainee's teeth. Schindler breaks down. He speaks about all the money he wasted, feeling guilty about all the lives he could have saved, had he been wiser and more selfless. The ring was inscribed in Hebrew,

"Whoever saves one life saves the entire world."

Every day, I watched money being thrown away in DCFS case management and juvenile court costs: legal fees for the state, legal fees for parents, tens of thousands in legal fees for parents filing complaints against the state, and concurrent state defense costs. I kept thinking that if that same money was channeled into the treatment fund, how many children could access it without losing their parents? If we kept one case out of juvenile court, would it help one child get treatment and keep his family? I kept envisioning Schindler standing before his flock, awash with guilt, saying, "This pin, two people. This is gold. Two more people. He would've given me two for it. At least one. He would've given me one. One more. One more person. A person, Stern. For this, I could've gotten one more person and I didn't."

More and more parents came to me asking for help. I did what I could to help them. I did save some families. Two moved out of state and received care for their kids they could not access in Illinois. I successfully steered others to resources that helped them in the nick of time. For many others, I was too late and they ended up in juvenile court facing neglect charges, as we did. How many did I help? I don't even know. I will always wonder if I could have saved just one more.

I often wonder where the outrage is. Who, at the state or local governments will accept blame or admit shame for victimizing mentally ill children and their parents? More importantly, which, if any, are willing to rectify it? When will custody relinquishment for mental healthcare be abolished?

> *"Thou shalt not be a victim. Thou shalt not be a perpetrator. Above all, thou shalt not be a bystander."*
> Holocaust Museum, Washington, DC

"I have not failed; I have just found 10,000 ways that do not work."

Thomas Edison

Chapter Nineteen

JOURNEY TO ADVOCACY

BACK IN HIGH SCHOOL, I was the geeky, shy kid. If my classmates had to vote on which one of us was to become one of the leading mental health advocates for children in our state, they certainly would not have chosen me. Along my journey in fighting the system, people have used a lot of adjectives to describe me; a loving mother who is also passionate, caring, dedicated, tenacious, unrelenting, courageous, bold, fearless, and probably some other words not nearly as flattering. I've been labeled a criminal, an outcast, a leader, a champion, a system warrior, and a pioneer. Depending upon whom you talk to, I'm the villain or the hero. I've since left the shy girl in the shadows. Regarding the geek girl inside of me, let's just say I've decided to embrace her. Overarching, I've discovered that deepest passions emerge when the very core of your fundamental beliefs are tested.

The experiences of our lives make up the fiber of who we really are. I wasn't born a fighter, but by virtue of surviving an erratic childhood, the fighter comes out when I get kicked to the curb. The negative in growing up that way is that when it comes to relationships, you tend to build protective walls around yourself. The positive side is that you become an independent thinker. When so many people in your life have let you down, you begin to rely on your own understanding. By virtue of having those experiences, I was able to open my mind to new ways of thinking, one of which was homeschooling.

Individualized Thinking

When our children were small, we attended a Baptist based church. Within that congregation, there were a lot of homeschooling families, even before it was fashionable to do so. Initially, I was fascinated and intrigued by the idea of homeschooling, but it was never something I saw myself doing. When the younger boys began to struggle with school in public settings, I began to think about it a lot more. As it turned out, it was one of the best choices that we made for the boys. Homeschooling yielded an unexpected benefit for me as teacher/mom. In teaching subjects on multi-grade levels, I learned more about elementary and high school academics than I had when I was a student myself. One of the things we studied at length was the formation and workings of our government.

Homeschooling gave me the opportunity not only to spend more time teaching the kids about civic duties and the government, but also to help them experience it. For two years of our homeschooling journey, my husband worked as a traveling carpenter. We spent 2 years traveling with him, living, schooling, and working on the road. It is my ability to be an individual thinker combined with our experiences in homeschooling that has helped me give this issue the scope that it demands. At various points along the journey, others encouraged me to embrace systematic thinking. It was my willingness to weigh the right thing against the usual thing that kept me out of the box of systematic thinking.

A New Pattern for Government

Among other things, we learned that our founding fathers analyzed every other type of government that existed at the time, to find that every one of them had an imbalance of power. The framers of our Constitution spent a lot of time praying and debating about forming a government that was democratic and just. They sought one that was vastly different than the ones they'd escaped and would offer the citizens a fair shake. They tenaciously sought a way to balance the power, knowing that too much power in the hands of one entity always led to societal downfall. They succeeded by forming three separate branches of government, with three separate functions, each balancing the other's power. Such a government had never been tried before.

Even though we have the best and most effective government in the world, one of the deficits is that once a law is passed, distinct channels form, which become outdated and ineffective as society changes. When there are no concurrent attempts to modify the channel in keeping with the law's original intents and purposes, laws become counterproductive. Author, Barbara Seuling, wrote a book called "You Can't Eat Peanuts in Church and Other Little-Known Laws" which is chock full of outdated laws which have never been amended or taken off the books. While the book is filled with humorous trivia, the concept is a fitting example of how circumstances can change over time to make something ridiculous out of something that once made so much sense. Not only should laws be formed with the end goal in mind, they must be continually monitored and periodically amended for effectiveness and validity. Some years ago, the wraparound mental health concept was a new idea that has yet to be developed to its full extent.

Wraparound in Infancy

A Chicago icon by the name of Karl Dennis is a long time promoter of wraparound. He is now retired, but in his prime, he was Executive Director of Kaleidoscope, one of the most innovative therapeutic foster care agencies ever in existence. Instead of mirroring existing programs, Karl and his associates developed a new philosophy designed around what they had all learned during their tenure as social workers. They arrived at three key concepts:

1. When children ran, they always ran home.
2. If you listen, families will tell you what they need.
3. They would not refuse anyone, no matter how bad the situation was.

They decided that instead of putting everyone in the same box with the same procedures and protocols, they'd approach each situation individually based upon the outcome they desired to see. Karl broadly defines the word wraparound as "doing whatever it takes." Stabilizing families meant identifying the end goal and formulating a path to successfully get there.

Residential vs. In-Home Care

During my advocacy efforts for my own son, I felt at odds with some of the other grass roots team members, who were part of the movement that I helped start. While I was advocating for my son to get residential treatment, other advocates were hesitant to align with me for fear of encouraging a warehousing movement, in which kids never returned back into the community.

I don't foresee a time when residential centers will cease to exist. There will always be a contingency of people that will require residential treatment. At the same time, I will qualify my insistence that state mental health systems included residential care as part of the overall plan. This intensive treatment should be reserved for people whose behavior or other mental healthcare needs cannot be safely managed in a family or group community setting. Preferably, the residential center would be in close proximity to the family's home so that they may visit regularly. The residential treatment should be continually geared towards returning the child home or moving him to the least restrictive community setting.

Residential treatment centers should be closely monitored to ensure that residents receive personal daily care, sufficient and healthy food, as well as making sure they are not overly sedated, secluded, or restrained. In addition, centers should be monitored to optimize educational and vocational opportunities.

Aftercare is almost as important as in-patient care so that the resident can successfully maintain stabilization within his home and community. In our experience, a lot of the hospitals and other centers said that they had aftercare programs, but not one of them helped us to put one into place. I promote the inclusion of residential care in mental health care reform, because our son was one whose behavior could not safely be managed at home, even with an extensive wraparound program in place.

When communities have a continuum of in-home and community based services available for the people that need them, they are less likely to end up in residential care, or may need it for a shorter period of time.

Technology is our biggest ally. When children need placements that are geographically distant from their homes, emails, teleconferencing, and video conferencing are family therapy's best friend. I anticipate technology based therapies will someday be the norm.

Families often ask me, "How do you know when your child needs to be in a residential center? How do you know when it's time to trade custody rights (not that anyone should have to)?" It's a very personal and difficult answer to either question. I share the knowledge and experience that I have, in order to help them make the best decision for themselves. That said; it generally boils down to one large issue-*safety.*

Identifying the Root of the Problem

In determining where the problem of custody relinquishment went all wrong, I had to figure out where it started. In order to begin solving any problem, the first step is to recognize the fact that problem exists. Excepting extremely rare instances, the state and federal governments are not likely to do this on their own. It really takes concerned United States citizens to bring the issues to the table for discussion and resolution. The next step to solving the problem is to create awareness regarding the issue. This important step is often overlooked. Because a problem is so all-consuming to you, it is easy to fall into a trap of assuming that it is equally pressing to others. You may gain sympathy or even empathy, but until the message reaches others in a meaningful way, their sense of urgency will never begin to equal the weight of yours. So, exactly how do you go about translating the issue to others in governmental bodies who are in a position to address it?

Begin by dissecting the root of the problem. Where did it start? How did it come about? What precipitated it? What aggravated it? How did it expand? Whom did it affect? What problems did it fix? What other problems arose incidentally as a result? How did it manifest or perpetuate itself over time? What attempts were made to change it? To thwart it? To stop it? What obstacles stood in the way then? What obstacles exist now?

Once you have the answers to those questions, you will begin to form the landscape of the problem. Solutions will become visible, if not glaring. At the same time, what solves one issue may create additional and greater problems. New and unexpected problems surface when failing to project how the changes will play out in the real world, especially if the plan does not include long term plan monitoring. This is why it is important to consider scope as it pertains to the present as well as the future.

Formulate Possible Solutions

The next step is to formulate thoughts about what it will take to fix it. Tap all available resources and collect data to support your findings. In analyzing this issue, I had to find applicable laws and analyze why they weren't effective. In Illinois, I discovered that there were two laws which were commonly applied in psychiatric lockout situations: the Juvenile Court Act and Minor Requiring Authoritative Intervention. After reading them, I asked attorneys and others within the court system how these laws were interpreted and applied. In doing this, it occurred to me that the reason the laws were not working towards this end was because they were never designed for this purpose. It was like putting the square peg in the round hole. It just never fit. Enact appropriate laws to appropriate situations. We need new laws that address psychiatric lockouts in ways that don't criminalize children or parents.

Advocate for Change

Once you have found the origin of the problem and analyzed the potential solutions, it's time to work towards resolving the issue. This is ostensibly the most difficult part of advocacy. It's the place where the rubber meets the road and the place where most advocates throw in the towel. It's a tall throw to land on the top of the heap of towels already tossed aside by other advocates. It is no small feat to rearrange the thinking of stubborn bureaucrats who cave to systematic thinking. My personal challenge was to get my feet out of the psychiatric revolving door and into the bureaucratic door. Naively, I thought it was a matter of calling my legislators. In truth, it would take an entire grass roots movement to get it moving. But what exactly does that mean?

Initially, the state senator took a few steps to try to help us. He assigned us a legislative liaison and made some calls to the state capitol. He introduced us to the Community and Residential Services Authority and asked for regular updates on progress or lack thereof. We had custody of our son at the onset of the first phone call. Just a few short months later, we lost custody of him at a shelter care hearing. Our senator could not interfere with the court system and could not help us retain or regain custody of our son. What he could do, was propose amendments to existing laws and propose new laws. Ultimately, he met in person, with several adoptive parents facing the same dilemma. It was at this breakfast meeting that he realized the full scope of the problem and agreed to help.

He was very honest with us in that meeting. He shared with us that virtually every recent legislative conversation centered on the fact that the state was billions of dollars in debt and that this was not likely to change in the foreseeable future. He expressed concern that any attempts he could make to amend the current system, were likely to be thwarted by a fiscal note that was doomed to defeat. He suggested that it would take a full-fledged grass roots movement to realize the sort of change that we were seeking.

Forming a grass roots movement turned out to be good advice. To be effective, a grass roots movement must include affected persons, not for profit organizations with a vested interest in the issue, and yes, even governmental officials and state departments. The legislator suggested a few groups that might be interested in joining our cause, so I started by contacting them. I started with organizations that focused on child mental health, foster care, adoption, and family issues. Most either knew about the issue or were interested in learning more about it. Some of them referred me to even more organizations or spread the word and others contacted me and an advocacy group was born. Technology is what helped me connect with parents all across Illinois, as well as in other states.

"He's My Son"

My outreach to parents began quite by accident with a five minute video that I put together based on a random thought. Most people recognize it by the title, "He's My Son." After Nebraska's Safe Haven debacle, Nebraska families formed A.S.K. or Alphabet Soup Kids, which has carried on the legacy of working with state departments and legislators toward positive change for mental health care in that state. A.S.K. has taken a strong pro-mental health and anti-custody relinquishment stance, providing strong support and guidance for Nebraska families.

During the Nebraska Safe Haven debacle, we got calls and emails from parents all over the country, asking us about our ordeal in Illinois, which had happened just six months prior. Many of the parents were from Nebraska. I opened my email one day to find that one of them, who was a hair's breath away from being forced to relinquish her son for mental healthcare, had sent me a song called, "He's My Son," by Mark Schultz. She simply said, "You have to hear this song, but make sure you have the tissues handy. Tears streaming, I listened to it over and over. Each time, pictures began to form in my mind to match the phrases. I wondered how I could show others what I could see in my mind's eye. And then I had a thought. I wondered how slide sharing worked. I opened that program and explored it. I made one slide, then two, then more. The pictures I'd seen in my mind began to tell a story. The final piece was to add the music. It was complete. I showed it to a few people. They were immensely moved and told me I couldn't keep it to myself. The rest of the world needed to hear our story and this was the way to do it. It told a very complicated, but compelling and emotional story in the space of five minutes. Another parent uploaded it on an internet sharing site. It spread virally. I received comments from viewers in many states, Canada, and even Australia. People were electronically sending it to each other. I accepted invitations to present it for legislators and state departments in Nebraska and Illinois, as well as for many other groups. The reaction was always the same. The room got starkly quiet while viewers choked back tears, some unsuccessfully. People describe this work as moving and compelling.

After the video made the rounds, I started my blog called Scope and Circumstance. It is a blog which has an extremely narrow focus, dedicated to children whose adoptive parents were forced into relinquishing custody for treatment. The link is www.scopeandcircumstance.wordpress.com. Parents email me, telling me their stories, and asking for help. Many joined the ranks as advocates. As this movement grew, I couldn't help but feel a bit envious of my Nebraska friends. They'd made allies with their legislators and state departments. They hadn't been able to abolish custody relinquishment either, but at least they were working on it. I needed to find a way to get the same kind of focus started in Illinois.

Sometimes we lost support from places we fully expected to gain it and gained support in other places we never even looked for it. We learned that some of the not for profit organizations which had leveraged advocacy efforts in the past, also had contracts or at least formidable ties with some of the state departments. While these organizations supported us privately, they declined to support us judicially and publicly, favoring to influence governmental departments behind the scenes. One such organization had trained us in trauma therapy for our son. When we sought their court support for obtaining trauma treatment for our son, they gently informed us that they would not publicly align with us as not to lose their large contract with DCFS. They exempted any affiliation with us once we locked horns with DCFS, over obtaining trauma treatment for our son. The adoptive parent support group we'd been attending disbanded as a result. After this unfortunate event, and during our quest to right the wrongs that had been inflicted upon us, as we were being categorically separated from our son, virtually every source of support that we'd gained along the way disappeared.

When we finally came to the conclusion that our son's treatment was covered under the EPSDT provision of Medicaid, and we never should have lost custody to begin with, along with other advocates, I explained it to the state departments in a large open forum. Once again, we were denied treatment, even though our son was legally entitled to it. We made a very important decision.

We filed a federal lawsuit against two of our state departments.

A Federal Lawsuit

ACMHAI discovered that we intended to file a federal lawsuit against the state. They suggested that notifying the governor's office directly of our plans would fare better for us than having them hear about it from another source.

I called the governor's policy advisor the same day. I told him that my son had spent his first few years in foster care. It was not our fault, nor his, that he'd been deprived of his permanency, which was awarded to him in juvenile court as a toddler, in exchange for the treatment he so badly needed. He was entitled to his treatment under the law, in fact, under a Medicaid card that he was awarded at the time he became a member of our family. I intended to see that he got it. He was 15 years old. He began his childhood in foster care. If I had any way of preventing it, he wasn't going to end it there.

The shy, geeky girl called the highest office in the state to inform them that she intended to file a federal lawsuit against the state to get her son's treatment covered under the EPSDT provision of Medicaid.

We filed it on a Wednesday evening. By the next morning, news of it spread from Springfield to Chicago within four hours of the start of the work day and discussions about it continued throughout the weekend.

After the lawsuit was filed, the state departments avoided us, the dividing lines were drawn, and we were thrown out of the advocacy arena. My formerly busy advocacy life came to a complete halt. The phone stopped ringing. The email box was empty. We were slightly demoralized and mildly muted. When our entire world went quiet, the National Alliance on Mental Illness (NAMI) coaxed us out of hiding.

NAMI

I had heard about a Criminal Justice Action Group that had recently formed and was operating under the NAMI umbrella. I had a couple of reasons for wanting to check it out. First, I suspected there was no one to lead parents who had issues in the juvenile court system. Perhaps I could use our experiences in the court to help. Second, our son had spent half his teen years as a ward of the state and living in residential centers. In all that time, he had not improved. Our worries over getting him stabilized were increasing. I decided it was time to pave the way for a future time when we might be facing adult court with him. Other parents were sadly at that place now. They would teach us from their experiences. Maybe it would help us do it better. Perhaps its only purpose was to help us endure it when the time came. Besides, now that no one else was talking to me, I suddenly had a lot more free time.

The NAMI members wanted to hear our story. They were outraged at what had happened to us and at what was happening to other parents like us. They wanted to know more. I was afraid to get too close. We'd been burned so many times. They wanted to help and gently prodded me. Through the silence, I'd lost some of my advocacy steam. Slowly, I made my way back to the advocacy forefront. I took the NAMI Family to Family course. A local NAMI affiliate, the NAMI Barrington Area affiliate, voted me onto their board. I decided to chair the Children's Advocacy Committee. As a member of NAMI, there was no fear of them leaving me because they weren't financially tied to anyone else. I felt supported and liberated. Not only were there no limitations to advocacy, they encouraged me to advance my cause and offered to help it along. NAMI had picked us up from the depths and given us back something we desperately needed, hope. Hundreds of caring arms wrapped around us once again.

At that first NAMI meeting, one of the board members was talking about how the first mental health court in Illinois got started. It was started by one person. That woman kept solemnly repeating, "One person. It was started by one person." At the onset of the meeting, I'd been feeling very alone in my advocacy efforts, but I left that meeting saying to myself, "I am one person. I am one person who can make a difference." Even if no one joined me, I was still one person. But I was not the only one affected and I was not alone. The movement swelled.

Chapter Twenty

CONCLUSION

WHEN DANIEL WAS 2 YEARS OLD, I made a commitment to him to be his mother for whatever period of time he needed me to be. When he was 4 years old, I made a commitment to be his mother for a lifetime. When he was 13 years old, I made the Devil's Deal to give him a chance at healing from the trauma he sustained prior to officially becoming my son. It was a contract that never needed to be drawn up. My husband and I made a commitment to be his parents and stand by him for the rest of his life. We kept our promise to love and support him unconditionally even when the government broke its promise to all of us.

Many people in society believe that people with mental illness have an "ick factor." As a family, we have experienced stigma to the largest degree possible. Even government officials working in healthcare and human services asked us why we would even take "those kids." They asked me, in a politically correct way, why I was working so hard to get treatment and custody of a throw-away.

More than a decade ago, during the time we were exploring the process of adoption, a well-meaning adoptive parent gave us some unanticipated advice. He told us not to take a biracial child. Those were the kids to stay away from because neither race wanted to call them their own. They didn't wholly fit into either culture. His advice struck us as odd. If we weren't willing to take them, who would? Who was supposed to love the biracial children? Who is supposed to love the mentally ill children? Those who are imperfect? The outcasts? The unlovable?

Our biggest fear in placing our son in a residential treatment center was that he might never come out. What if he could never safely live within a family setting? What if he was never able to return the love and affection towards us that we had for him? Should we sever that tie and leave his life in the hands of people who are paid to care for him? Does mental illness make him unworthy of being loved by his family? Should we never visit him or celebrate his birthdays and other special milestones? Should he cease being part of our family dynamic? Some government officials and other professionals suggested that, yes, in those instances, ties should be severed.

If that is the case, then permanency through adoption is a fallacy. It's not permanent. It's conditional. The philosophy of permanency is based upon the degree of mental illness, drawing a firm line between those who can live in a family setting and those who can't. As long as adoption is conditional or episodic based upon mental illness, I suggest we just leave them in foster care. For a child to grieve over the loss of parents once, is devastating enough. It is cruel to force emotionally compromised children to endure it twice.

Parents of developmentally disabled children, who are residentially placed, love and visit their children. Parents of imprisoned children visit them while they are incarcerated. Who would deny either of those parents the right to parent their children? Why then, are we allowing it in regards to mentally ill children?

What about the fallout to the rest of the family? The family is stuck in the hard parts of grief with no hope of emotional healing for themselves, oppressed into a hopeless situation. In order to keep their commitments to their children, they must endure deep scrutiny under the "abuse lens" and subsequent criminalization through juvenile court. When trading custody rights for mental healthcare, who really wins? Certainly not the child nor the family. Perhaps we should leave the children in foster care.

When trying to access treatment for our son, we felt like a ping pong ball. We called one state department which denied funding and sent us to another state department, which also denied funding and sent us to another, etc., until we arrived at the starting point and began the process all over again. The system will remain broken until the departments synergize and work together to find ways to fund care, rather than finding ways to get out of funding it.

As long as systems have no checks and balances, abuses of power will infect the process. Children and families, already severely stressed and broken, under threats of "cooperation," cave to child welfare and judicial demands, driving them further into oppression, causing risk of family dissolution. In one of the statewide agency meetings I attended, a DCFS manager complained vocally that parents give up, leaving DCFS stuck to be parents to our children. I offered to provide him with an explanation as to why that happens. He didn't make himself available to hear the answer, which is to stop attacking them and start supporting them. I sent him an email explaining why they give up. He didn't respond. By denying families treatment options that will keep them together despite dealing with a severe emotional disorder, I throw the question right back to the state departments. Who gave up?

What about the morality of it all? Why are mentally ill children given less services than physically ill children? Is it not embarrassing enough that people gawk and stare at us when our children act up in public settings? Is it not painful enough that other children don't want to play with them because they are different and undesirable? Are we not isolated enough just trying to carry on normal day to day activities? Does the government really need to cap it all off by humiliating and criminalizing the parents after denying appropriate assistance?

What will it take to fix it? What will it take to provide treatment and family preservation without question? Should parents wear orange jumpsuits and a green mental health awareness ribbon to court appearances and administrative case reviews? Should we stand a mother and child on an auction block and have onlookers gawk as DCFS sends the child to treatment and the parents to court? I certainly hope that it will not take such drastic steps to get the point across, but I sometimes fear that it will.

Preferably, we can form a task force of child mental health stakeholders, including parents, and redesign a system in which second time foster children cease to exist. Abolish the barbaric practice of trading custody rights for care. The families are committed to system reform, but are the governments ready for us?

The least detrimental alternative is to stunt a child in foster care, leaving him as a first time foster child, sparing him the agony of becoming a second time foster child.

The most favorable outcome is to lead the child and family to appropriate mental health services with full support from the clinical team. Families need strong support to endure the challenges and hardships that are inherent in dealing with mental illness. Dividing children and families, while isolating children and attacking parents, leads to familial instability, disruption, and dissolution.

Somewhere towards the beginning of the journey, I attempted to arrange a meeting between the deputy directors of DCFS and adoptive families to work together towards positive reform. I was met with, "Mrs. Hoy, who do you think you are to demand such an audience?"

Who is Toni Hoy? I suppose I am different things to different people.

I was the kind of mom who played with my kids every day. There was too much of the world to experience to waste time watching television. During our homeschool years, our kids complained that they never got a "snow day" as often happens in the Midwest. Yet "snow days" were my favorite days. It was a day for the kids to stay in their pajamas after eating warm pancakes and finish their homeschool work while sipping a steaming cup of hot cocoa. After shoveling out, it was time for making snow angels, building snow forts, sledding, and tossing snow into the air for our dog to chase. I miss "snow days" the most. I faced a fair amount of criticism in our early homeschool days, but I don't regret a moment of time I spent with my kids during those years, and my kids remember those days fondly as well.

The state departments have described me as passionate, tenacious, compelling, and a strong advocate. I was someone who wasn't afraid to say what needed to be said and didn't mince words. I was perhaps a bit of a thorn in their side. They were equally a thorn in mine. Perhaps one day we will meet in the rose garden. As I relayed to one of them:

> "The United States Marines are the first to go in and the last to come out. They are the bravest of the brave and the toughest of the tough. They don't leave a man behind. They don't quit! *And neither do the mothers who raised them.*"

Connections with other parents came to me from across the nation. We supported and encouraged one another. We grieved and cried together. We rejoiced together in our children's small steps of progress. We educated each other regarding our trials with trauma and the system. The parents might refer to me as a bulwark and fighter. I was often the voice of reason, a sounding board, a resource, an expert, and at least once, a hero.

My son, Daniel, would probably tell you that I am someone who "gets him." He would add by saying that I have the ability to "look beyond a brain disorder" and see who he really is. He'd continue by saying that you should never tick me off on haircut day. This book is a testimony to his struggle to regulate his emotions, so that he could do what most other people take for granted. Live a normal life. I don't want him to ever have a smidgeon of doubt that he's worth it.

Daniel's peers at the residential center would refer to me as the "cool mom." You know, the mom who even though she is a foot shorter than all of them, and stinks at basketball will shoot a few hoops with them anyway. I'm the mom who showed up every week without fail, with a smile on her face and a kind word for all of them, even the gang members. A conservatively dressed mom with a bit of an adventurous side, a dose of humor, and a tattoo on her foot. Amongst his peers, I have a reputation for being strict, but ultra-attentive, and fair, and one who has always had a heart for the underdog. I was the mom for whom the mother-less boys hoped would take notice of them, and adopt them too.

Ultimately, I'm someone in between a Madeleine Albright and a Leigh Anne Touhy, and if you're still not sure, just "read my pins."

> *"...I've learned the dignity of being loyal to something you believe in. Of holding onto it, above all else. Of believing, without question, that it will carry you home."*
>
> From the movie, "*The Soloist.*"

AFTERWORD

MORE THAN THREE YEARS after we were forced to abandon our youngest son at a psychiatric hospital, D.H. v. Illinois HFS and DHS was settled "to the satisfaction of the parties."

That same year, Michigan adoptive families filed Cole et al v. Snyder, a class action suit against their Governor and DHS, for failure to provide therapeutic treatment, according to their post-adoption subsidies. Immediately after it was filed, one of the families received full funding.

On August 26, 2011, the Chicago Tribune reported that Illinois DCFS Director, Erwin McEwen, resigned. The article highlighted accomplishments the Director had made during his tenure. According to the article, a DCFS agency spokesman said that "Mac," as he was called, was moving on to other opportunities and was not forced out. Two months later, the Chicago Tribune reported that Dr. George E. Smith had allegedly fraudulently received government grants of over 18 million dollars, millions which had been awarded to him by DCFS. DCFS and other state departments failed to monitor the grant monies awarded to Dr. Smith. The Office of Investigator General discovered that large amounts of the grant monies were spent on Chicago sporting events and other personal expenses, including alcohol, rather than on human services for children and families. While "Mac" denied funding to post-adoptive families for treatment, he failed to oversee millions in grant money to a man the media referred to as "his pal."

18 million dollars could have gone a long way towards creating a mental health infrastructure to support children and families. 18 million dollars

would have prevented all of the 104 families in 2010 from being forced into relinquishing custody of their children in exchange for mental healthcare. After reading those reports in the Chicago Tribune, I re-read many of the emails that other families had sent to me crying out for assistance in obtaining funding for their children's treatment. I was grievous and angry!

On September 29, 2011, N.B. v Illinois HFS was filed in Illinois federal court. This suit, not only alleged violations of EPSDT, but also violations of ADA and the Rehabilitation Act. It also requested certification as class action on behalf of over 18,000 children with severe mental and emotional disorders.

Regaining Custody

I stood looking through my jewelry box, the morning of June 27, 2011, wondering which pin I should wear on my suit. Madeleine Albright's book, "Read My Pins: Stories from a Diplomat's Jewel Box" was released during our ordeal. I have always admired her and loved reading the fascinating stories of how she got her pins and the significance of the occasions that she wore them. Today was an important day. In a couple of hours, Randie, Jim, and I would appear before the judge with a petition to regain custody of our son. I stroked my finger over a square, silver pin. It has a really cool maze design that plays in the light. It is the logo of the Frank Lloyd Taliesin Fellowship. A year prior, I bought the maze pin in a little souvenir shop in Chicago, after my meeting at the Governor's office. I purchased it as a memento of that meeting because it reminded me of the complexity of the Illinois mental health system. Today was a fitting day to wear it. I pinned it onto my suit jacket and headed to court.

As we walked into the courtroom, we felt more like victors than the stinkin' parents. This case took a turn that the judges and attorneys never expected. Daniel continued to damage property and hurt people. Court professionals were all sure that he'd age out of the system at the age of 21, just like the GAL told us he would, on that very first day that I cried in the court lobby. It's fair to say that the attorneys and the judge were now quite *gobsmacked!* How did this little mom figure out the law, explain it to the government, settle a federal lawsuit in a mere seven months, and turn the whole mess around in just over three years? There was an unspoken admission that, while they were the ones charged with serving the child's "best interests," justice was ultimately served by a mother's boundless love for her son. There was an air of prudent surrender. It felt good to recapture our sense of dignity and we embraced it. The judge and state's attorney were ready to grant our petition favorably. Of course, every game of cards has a wild card and this time, it was the GAL.

The GAL, a fairly recent replacement of the original one, said that she really didn't have a problem with it, but wanted to speak with "her client" first. Randie informed her that "her client" was 5 ½ hours away. For a fleeting moment, I wondered if she even knew his name. The GAL grimaced at the notion of having to travel so far to interview him. Despite the judge asking her how and when she intended to accomplish the interview, the GAL insisted that she be allowed time to conduct it. We were not allowed to comment regarding the GAL's request for a final, private interrogation of our son. As usual, the GAL declined to speak with "her client's" parents to receive an update as to how he was doing. As we emotionally prepared to reunify our family, it was clear that some parties still perceived us as two separate entities. Though we unfailingly demonstrated our level of commitment to our son, right down to the final days, we were forced to tolerate, "Talk to the hand." The judge granted her request.

The GAL then turned to Randie and asked for a copy of the federal settlement agreement. We detected a hint of pride in Randie's voice, as she responded that the Attorney General ordered that the settlement agreement be filed under judicial seal. The only person with access to it—*was the judge.* Once again, the GAL frowned. For years, we had been forced to lay all of our cards on the table. It felt refreshing to finally be the bearer of the trump card, even though we played our final hand while remaining in the "accused" chairs.

The judge set a new court date, agreeing to waive our appearance. Randie thanked the judge for her consideration; however, we had learned not to take anything for granted. I clearly recalled one of our earliest court appearances, when a judge waived our requirement to appear. In our absence, DCFS sent a cut-throat attorney into court with intent to sabotage our no-fault dependency plea. Even though the judge did not require us to appear at that hearing, afterwards, the other attorneys, caseworkers, and CASA, vocally and openly questioned our commitment to our son. We would not make that mistake again. If there was a court date scheduled; we would be there, in person.

Shortly after we left the courthouse, it occurred to me that if the GAL didn't know that Daniel was 5 ½ hours away, she surely didn't know that she wasn't going to find him at the residential treatment center. After a recent psychiatric crisis, in which the law became involved, Daniel was being detained at the juvenile detention center. Instinctively, I reached into my purse for the GAL's phone number with intent to give her the number to the detention center. As I pulled her card from my purse, I paused for a moment, to ponder if she would have granted me the same consideration. I recalled my first encounter with her, shortly after she was assigned to the case. I sat next to her in the courtroom, but she refused to acknowledge me. After the hearing, I stood next to her and paused so that I could introduce myself. She refused to look up at me. Decisively, I dropped her business card back into my purse, tossing it onto the passenger seat of my car. She could track him down herself.

I walked around the mall for a while to de-stress before returning to the office. At a major department store, the table of brooches drew me in. I enjoyed browsing through them, relating their meanings to my life, just as Madeleine Albright did. Ah! As soon as I saw it, I knew the one I would buy. It was a heart shaped pin with a large pink butterfly. That was me and Jim, about to be set free. A smaller butterfly flew above it. That was Daniel, also, about to be free. Stars encircled the butterflies. We had certainly risen to the heavens.

The next two weeks could not go fast enough. The GAL did not travel 5 ½ hours to visit "her client." In fact, while she stymied our petition to regain the guardianship we never should have lost; she didn't even bother to call him herself. She assigned her assistant to interrogate him. We inquired of Daniel as to what she asked him. Among other things, the GAL's assistant wished to know if Daniel knew what his parents were doing. He affirmed that he was well aware of our petition to regain custody of him. She asked whether he would feel "safe" with his parents as his guardian rather than DCFS and GAL. Daniel quickly replied, "Yes." Daniel confided in me that he learned through experience, to answer GAL, CASA, and DCFS questions without hesitation. Any time spent thinking about a question, was generally followed by many more questions. Short, to-the-point answers usually ended the interrogation sooner than well thought out answers.

Even in the 11th hour, the GAL continued to see us as abusive parents, failing to consider:

- Daniel was interviewed while being detained in juvenile detention for assaulting an elderly, health impaired teacher, from behind her back.
- We had never abused or neglected Daniel.
- Daniel had not even lived in our home for over three years due to his violence towards his family and others, and was not set for discharge in the foreseeable future.
- It was a no-fault dependency case, not an abuse or neglect case.

We returned to the Depke Juvenile Court, two weeks later, to try once again for return of custody. I wore the butterfly pin that I purchased weeks before, fairly certain that this was the day that we would all be set free. Seconds before we entered the courtroom, the DCFS caseworker approached us. "Why are we here? What is going on? I don't know anything. Something about a lawsuit or something. You probably want to get rid of us. People don't like us. You will probably be happy to get rid of us."

I don't generally have patience for incompetence, so I glanced at my feet to mask my feelings of distaste. Randie knew this was her cue to speak on my behalf. I marveled at how in tune we had become with each other through this. We became like the ebb and flow of the tide. She instinctively knew just when to take over. It took me a little longer to catch on, but I finally learned when to recede and let her take the lead. I don't even remember how she responded to him. I didn't need to know. I trusted her.

We entered the courtroom and sat in the "accused" chairs. This time, I sat down directly, not bothering to acknowledge the GAL's presence. The hearing began. The judge asked if there was any objection to our petition to regain custody of our son. The GAL piped up and noted that her assistant had spoken to Daniel, however; he was not even at the residential center when she called. The residential center referred her to speak with him at the juvenile detention center. She followed that remark by saying she had no objection. The judge thanked her.

The judge turned to us and said that she hoped that Daniel would get better. I responded by saying that we'd stand by him either way.

"I know you will!" she said, "Good luck to all of you."

Jim and I regained custody of our son, Daniel, on July 14, 2011, in a hearing that lasted all of about 60 seconds. We arose from the "accused" chairs for the final time and exited the courtroom without engaging with anyone. Randie, alone, congratulated us in the lobby. Our painful ordeal culminated in victory after three years and four months of unnecessary trauma. *It was finally over.* We stood in the lobby for a moment to let it all sink in. The emotion engulfed both of us, but this time, the tears hit Jim's eyes before mine. We cried in the court lobby on the first day and the last.

Later that evening, we phoned Daniel in the detention center. Jim said, "Daniel, WE ARE YOUR PARENTS!" He let out a shriek of utter joy, "REALLY?!" It was the happiest moment of all.

The residential center requested that we complete a new stack of admission forms, since DCFS no longer had guardianship of Daniel. Jim and I took complete pleasure in signing all 48 pages on the lines marked "Parent or Guardian." We copied them so that Daniel could see that there was no DCFS stamp to be found anywhere.

The long awaited reunification day had finally arrived. Had the right thing been done from the start, there would be no cause for celebration. I wish God had seen fit to let us wallow in our victory, at least for a bit, but it was not to be. Our triumph was bittersweet. The day after we signed the agreement, in a fit of rage, our son had broken some laws, landing him in juvenile detention. In just one short month, we'd be walking through the metal detector of a different juvenile court to attend his sentencing hearing. We took solace in knowing that, this time, his case was there for the right reasons. This time, the only two people who'd be representing his parents, were the two people that should have been doing it all along—his very own mother and father.

During our ordeal, the monies that the state expended to pursue us in juvenile court and administrative law court, as well as to defend against us in federal court, would have paid for a large portion of Daniel's treatment. No amount of money could ever compensate us for the profound emotional suffering, grief, and loss that we all sustained through this incredibly painful ordeal.

Daniel continues to work on emotional stability. Our family, as a unit, continues to work on emotional healing.

REFERENCES

Department of Children and Family Services, Illinois. "Adoption." 2009. <http://www.state.il.us/dcfs/adoption/index.shtml>.

Department of Children and Family Services, Illinois. "Putting it All Together: A Handbook for Children." November 2009. <http://www.state.il.us/dcfs/docs/CFS%201050-d70%20Putting%20it%20all%20Together.pdf>.

Department of Health Services. "Eligibility Criteria for the Individualized Care Grant." <http://www.dhs.state.il.us/page.aspx?item=33654>.

Eich, Dominique and Bernd Figner. "Having Attention-Deficit/Hyperactivity Disorder and Substance Use Disorder: A Review of the Literature," Zurich University Hospital, Zurich, Switzerland. < http://www.columbia.edu/~bf2151/eich_figner.pdf>.

Graham, Cathleen S. "Implementation of the Adoptive and Safe Families Act of 1997:

"The Juvenile Court Process." Illinois State Bar Association. < http://www.illinoislawyerfinder.com/legalinfo/2007/01/juv_court_process.html>.

The Indiana Experience" Advances in Social Work, Volume 1, No. 1, Spring (2000) http://journals.iupui.edu/index.php/advancesinsocialwork/article/viewFile/104/94.

North Carolina Division of Social Services and the Family and Children's Resource Program. Practice Notes. Volume 6, Number 2, May, 2001. "African American Children in Foster Care." http://www.practicenotes.org/vol6_no2/cspn%20v6_2.pdf.

The History Place. "Genocide in the 20th Century." 2000. http://www.historyplace.com/worldhistory/genocide/holocaust.htm.

U.S. Department of Health and Human Resources. "EPSDT and Title V Collaboration to Improve Child Health." < http://www.hrsa.gov/epsdt/overview.htm>.

Wexler, Richard. "Take the Child and Run: Tales from the Age of ASFA." National Coalition for Child Protection Reform. < http://www.nccpr.org/reports/asfa.pdf

GLOSSARY

ACMHAI—Association of Community Mental Health Authorities of Illinois, a partnership of Illinois community mental health boards.

ACR—Administrative case review, an independent review process required by federal and state law in Illinois, administered by child welfare, with the goal of ensuring safety, well-being, and permanency for children in foster care.

ADHD—attention deficit disorder, a child or adult with some combination of symptoms of inattention, hyperactivity, and impulsivity.

Adjudication—as it pertains to juvenile court, a judgment of a child's permanency ruling, which might include return home, independence, adoption, foster care, or guardianship.

Adoption Preservation Unit—a unit within the child welfare department dedicated to preserving adoptions that they formed.

ASFA—the Adoptive and Safe Families Act, signed into law by President William Clinton in 1997. The law was intended to move foster children into permanent adoptive homes.

A.S.K.—Alphabet Soup Kids, a group of parents, primarily in Nebraska, dedicated to child mental health advocacy and family support, which arose from the 2008 Nebraska Safe Haven Debacle.

AWOL—absent without leave.

Bipolar disorder—a disorder that causes periods of mania alternating with periods of depression.

CARES—24 hour crisis and service referral helpline in Illinois.

CANTS—child abuse and neglect tracking system.

CAPTA—Child Abuse Prevention and Treatment Act, also called the Mondale Act, was enacted in 1974 and has been amended several times. It created mandated reporters and mandated minimum standards for neglect and abuse of children.

CASA—court appointed special advocate, volunteers appointed by the court to be the "eyes and ears" for the judge and to be the child's voice in court. They are trained in neglect and abuse cases.

CAYIT—child and youth investment team, a team of DCFS workers, child and family members who convene to make placement decisions regarding the child.

CD—conduct disorder, which involves chronic behavior problems including defiance, impulsivity, and other anti-social behavior.

CERAP—child endangerment risk assessment protocol, a caseworker tool which consists of a list of 14 questions, which indicate the existence or absence of child endangerment risk factors.

CRSA—Community and Residential Services Authority, an Illinois state authority which aids families in obtaining services for children, under the age of 21, with severe emotional disorders and other behavioral disorders.

CWLA—Child Welfare League of America, a partnership of public and private agencies committed to promoting the safety, well-being, and permanency of children, youth, and their families.

DCFS—the Department of Children and Family Services, a state agency that bears the responsibility for protecting children.

DuPuy vs. Samuels—a court case which expedited cases of child abuse allegations for child care workers. The same case proved that DCFS falsely indicates parents in 75% of cases.

Educational surrogate—a surrogate appointed by DCFS to sign for a state ward's educational needs.

EMDR—eye movement desensitization and reprocessing, a specific treatment for post-traumatic stress disorder, which mimics rapid eye movement during sleep.

EPSDT—early, periodic, screening, diagnostic, and treatment, a provision of federal Medicaid law which provides for early screening for children so that services may be put into place before problems become extensive. It mandates treatment that is medically necessary.

Expunged—when a record ceases to exist as when parent's names are removed from the child abuse registry.

FASD—fetal alcohol spectrum disorder, a disorder manifested in utero which damages a fetus' brain due to a pregnant mother drinking alcohol during her pregnancy.

GAL—guardian ad litem, an attorney appointed by the court to represent the child.

Generation Y— people born in the mid 1980's and later, also called the millenials.

HFS—Healthcare and Family Services, Illinois Medicaid program.

ICG—Individualized Care Grant, through the Department of Human Services, a grant for severely mentally ill children to cover some of the costs on community based or residential care.

IEP—Individualized Educational Plan, an individualized educational plan written to meet the educational needs of children with special education needs.

Juvenile Court Act—a law which outlines the conditions and parameters for abuse, neglect, and dependency cases in juvenile court.

Lockout—when a parent refuses to allow a child back into their home.

LSD—Lysergic acid diethylamide, a popular street drug in the 1970's and 1980's, commonly referred to as acid.

Medicaid—United States health program for persons with low income and resources.

NAMI—National Alliance on Mental Illness, a not for profit advocacy organization for mentally ill persons with chapters at the national, state, and local levels.

OCD—obsessive compulsive disorder, an anxiety disorder where people have unwanted and repetitive thoughts, feelings, ideas, and sensations and behaviors that drive them to perform certain tasks, rituals, or other actions.

ODD—oppositional defiant disorder, a persistent pattern of tantrums, arguing, and angry or disruptive behaviors toward others, especially authority figures.

OIG—Office of Investigator General, a state department that investigates misconduct and rule violations by DCFS employees, foster parents, service providers and DCFS contractors.

Post-Adopt—A department within DCFS dedicated to services for families with finalized DCFS adoptions, also called Adoption Preservation.

PRTF—psychiatric residential treatment facility, any non-hospital facility with a provider agreement with a State Medicaid Agency to provide the inpatient services benefit to Medicaid-eligible individuals under the age of 21, subject to certain governmental rules.

PTSD—post traumatic stress disorder, an anxiety disorder which develops after an event to someone who experiences grave physical harm or a life threatening experience, such as rape, physical attack, military combat, or severe neglect or abuse.

RAD—reactive attachment disorder, children who were not held, loved, nurtured, and given physical care at the earliest stages of development, from pre-birth and before ages 3–5 years old. They become incapable of forming healthy attachments, lacking empathy for others and becoming physically aggressive towards people and property.

Rule #84—DCFS Illinois lockout rule which states the parameters that parents may or may not be indicated for neglect with regards to locking their child out of the house.

SACWIS—statewide automated child and welfare information system, an automated case management system for child welfare officials, which is funded by the federal government.

SASS—Screening, Assessment, and Support Services, a state department that serves children experiencing a mental health crisis and who may need mental health hospitalization.

SED—severe emotional disorder or serious emotional disturbance.

Shelter care hearing—a hearing for a minor who is delinquent or otherwise without parental supervision. The hearing must be held within 40 hours of the child being found, not including weekends and court designated holidays.

State Central Registry—a list of persons who were indicated in a child protection investigation.

Synergy—the whole is greater than the sum of the parts.

TEFRA—Tax Equity and Fiscal Responsibility Act, also known as the Katie Beckett option.

Voluntary Placement Agreement—an agreement between parents or guardians and the child welfare department for the state to take responsibility for care and placement of a child to access services that the parent or guardian is unable to access on their own.

ABOUT THE AUTHOR

Toni Hoy, a long time foster-adoptive parent, lives in the Chicago area, and makes a career as a licensed insurance agent. In 2011, Safeco Insurance selected her as the "Community Hero" and her employer, Hill and Stone Insurance Agency, Inc. presented the monetary award to NAMI on her behalf. As a leading child mental health advocate, she has made presentations before state departments and legislators in Illinois and Nebraska. She was interviewed on Madison, Wisconsin's WORT radio program, "Healthwriter" as well as a WBEZ radio program called "Out of the Shadows" in Chicago. As a free-lance writer, she has authored articles for the Family Defense Center newsletter and Rise Magazine. She chairs the Children's Advocacy Committee for NAMI Barrington Area affiliate, where she also serves on the Board of Directors. In addition, she authors a regular column for the NAMI Barrington Area newsletter called "In the Trench" and facilitates a family support group for parents and children. She earned a B.A. in Communications from Thomas Edison State College, New Jersey, and was a recipient of the Arnold

Fletcher Award for academic excellence. She and her husband, Jim, of 25 years have two biological children, two adoptive children, a daughter-in-law, and one foster son.

BUY A SHARE OF THE FUTURE IN YOUR COMMUNITY

These certificates make great holiday, graduation and birthday gifts that can be personalized with the recipient's name. The cost of one S.H.A.R.E. or one square foot is $54.17. The personalized certificate is suitable for framing and will state the number of shares purchased and the amount of each share, as well as the recipient's name. The home that you participate in "building" will last for many years and will continue to grow in value.

Here is a sample SHARE certificate:

YES, I WOULD LIKE TO HELP!

I support the work that Habitat for Humanity does and I want to be part of the excitement! As a donor, I will receive periodic updates on your construction activities but, more importantly, I know my gift will help a family in our community realize the dream of homeownership. **I would like to SHARE in your efforts against substandard housing in my community!** *(Please print below)*

PLEASE SEND ME _____ SHARES at $54.17 EACH = $ $_____

In Honor Of: _____

Occasion: (Circle One)   HOLIDAY   BIRTHDAY   ANNIVERSARY

      OTHER: _____

Address of Recipient: _____

Gift From: _____ *Donor Address:* _____

Donor Email: _____

I AM ENCLOSING A CHECK FOR $ $_____ PAYABLE TO HABITAT FOR HUMANITY <u>OR</u> PLEASE CHARGE MY VISA OR MASTERCARD *(CIRCLE ONE)*

Card Number _____ Expiration Date: _____

Name as it appears on Credit Card _____ Charge Amount $ _____

Signature _____

Billing Address _____

Telephone # Day _____ Eve _____

PLEASE NOTE: Your contribution is tax-deductible to the fullest extent allowed by law.
Habitat for Humanity • P.O. Box 1443 • Newport News, VA 23601 • 757-596-5553
www.HelpHabitatforHumanity.org

CPSIA information can be obtained
at www.ICGtesting.com
Printed in the USA
LVOW12s0319280917
550348LV00006B/968/P